Thomas William M. Marshall

Church Defence

Report of a Conference on the present Dangers of the Church

Thomas William M. Marshall

Church Defence

Report of a Conference on the present Dangers of the Church

ISBN/EAN: 9783337162634

Printed in Europe, USA, Canada, Australia, Japan

Cover: Foto ©ninafisch / pixelio.de

More available books at **www.hansebooks.com**

CHURCH DEFENCE:

Report of a Conference

ON THE

PRESENT DANGERS OF THE CHURCH.

"Here's neither bush nor shrub to bear off any weather at all, and another storm brewing; I hear it sing i' the wind."
Tempest, Act ii., sc. 2.

LONDON:
R. WASHBOURNE, 18, PATERNOSTER ROW.
1873.

MEMBERS OF THE CONFERENCE.

Canon Lightwood,
Archdeacon Tennyson,   } *Ritualists.*
Rev. Cyril Hooker,

The Regius Professor of Chaldee,
The Bishop of Dorchester,   } *High Churchmen.*
Rev. Prebendary Smiles,

The Bishop of Brighton,
Archdeacon Softly,   } *Low Churchmen.*
Rev. Silas Trumpington,

Dean Marmion,
Rev. Prebendary Creedless,   } *Broad Churchmen.*

Rev. Mark Weasel,....................   *Anglican Unattached.*

Scene of the Conference.
Dean Marmion's Library.

THE CONFERENCE.

Dean Marmion opened the proceedings. He need not disclaim any pretension to shape the discussion upon which they were about to enter. He was their host, but nothing more. It had seemed to him expedient at this crisis, of which they all recognised the gravity, to gather together representatives of the various schools of religious thought in their communion. They had accepted his invitation, and he thought they had done wisely. If they could arrive at any common principle of action in defending the National Church, of which they were all, in spite of wide differences of theological opinion, authorised pastors and official advocates, their discussion would not be barren. Their enemies were united, but *they* were not. Was it possible to remove this initial difficulty? This was the question which he submitted to their wisdom.

Mr. Weasel had accepted the invitation of the learned Dean, and did not regret having done so.

But he thought it important to define clearly, at the outset, *what* they were called upon to defend. There were four totally different Churches of England in that room, and a good many more outside it. Which of them was it proposed to defend?

The Professor of Chaldee (who was received with evident marks of interest) observed that he had yielded to the solicitation of valued friends, not without repugnance, in consenting to take part in this discussion. He desired that its fruits might be salutary. He was neither sanguine nor despondent. No man regretted more deeply than himself the unhappy divisions to which Mr. Weasel had referred, but they were nothing new. From the beginning this inconvenience had been felt in their own branch of the Church Catholic. That the English Church had continued, in spite of it, to discharge her providential mission, and to preach "the faith once delivered to the saints," was a manifest proof that God was with her. The evils which she had endured in the past she could endure now. Better strife than stagnation. He had no fears for the Church of England. She might cease to exist in her present form, and he had on many occasions admitted that certain contingencies might arise—such as the suppression of the Athanasian creed—which would make it a duty to depart from her. But if she fell, as even her friends seemed to anticipate, it would only be to live again in a new and more attractive form. The difficulty noticed by Mr. Weasel, however hardly it might press upon some sections of the clergy, was not felt by the Catholic portion of their community. Mr. Weasel appeared to be surprised at this observation, but it was easily explained. Anglo-Catholics were members, not simply of the English, but of the Universal Church. It was their duty to sympathise with the trials of a weak and ailing branch, and to "mourn with those who mourn," but their hopes and aspirations were not confined within its narrow boundary. Though it should cease to exist to-morrow, its Catholic children would not be without an altar and a home. Catholic prelates would be found to govern their flock, however diminished in number, and to perpetuate their priesthood. For this reason he saw nothing fatal in the objection of Mr. Weasel. In proposing to "defend the Church," he and his friends had in view a communion Catholic, though reformed, and of which the divisions, lamentable as they were, could not obscure the divine character. He thought, therefore, that on this basis they might combine, in spite of the difficulty suggested by Mr. Weasel, to frame a scheme of "Church Defence," and in this conviction he was ready to bear his part in the deliberations proposed by Dean Marmion.

PREBENDARY CREEDLESS (who addressed the meeting with a fluency and liveliness which seemed to imply considerable confidence in his own views), was glad that the eminent divine, whom they all respected, saw his way to concerted action among the different sections of their community. The announcement did not surprise him. He had never doubted that while their differences were sentimental and emotional, they were all of one mind in their first principles. (Vehement marks of dissent from Archdeacon Tennyson.) The Professor of Chaldee, perhaps inadvertently, had just proved it. In proclaiming that he and his friends were prepared, in certain very probable contingencies, to make a new Church, without consulting any authority whatever but their own tastes and predilections, he evidently agreed with Dean Marmion and himself, that a Church was a purely human institution, and that anybody could make a new one, whenever he felt impelled to do so.

THE PROFESSOR OF CHALDEE observed, with some severity of manner, that he had never thought of making a "new" Church, but only of reproducing the existing Anglican Church in a new form.

PREBENDARY CREEDLESS could more easily appreciate the subtle distinction, if the hypothetical failure of the Established Church had not been assumed as the very motive for creating a purer community. To abandon a Church because it had become unfaithful and defiled, transfer to a new one the allegiance of which it had ceased to be worthy, and yet maintain that they were still the *same* communion, appeared to him to approach the ideal limits of contradiction and absurdity. He knew that the school to which the Regius Professor belonged, and of which he was so distinguished a leader, contended that this was precisely what the Church of England had done in departing from the Church of Rome. No fundamental disparity of creed, they said, was implied in the separation, and they were still *one* Church. How firmly they believed their own theory was proved every day by their cordial attitude towards the sister church, and the remarkably amicable relations existing between them. (General laughter.) If there was anything in which High Church journals were now unanimous, it was in ceaseless vituperation of the Church of Rome, which their writers appeared to hate with an ardent animosity of which the ordinary old-fashioned Protestant was wholly incapable. The Anglican and Roman bodies, they were told, were integral parts of the same church, and he was quite willing to believe it if he could; but the birds lodged in their branches differed conspicuously in shape and plumage, and were chiefly occupied in pecking at each other. From early morn till the close of day, these vociferous birds uttered screams of mutual defiance which did not produce harmony of sound, and defended their respective nests with a clamorous ferocity which did not suggest unity of species. Even their callow broods could hardly be restrained from feeble and immature combats. To quit the region of metaphor, the habitual language of Ritualists towards Romanists, and their mutual reproaches, afforded the clearest proof that the former had no serious faith in their own technical theory. Only the other day, a High-church Bishop announced in a published document, addressed to the "Old Catholics" at Cologne, that the Church of Rome is now, and always had been, "heretical and schismatical." He evidently felt, as every man of sense must do, that only on some such supposition could the autonomy of the Church of England be justified—at least on High-church principles. But it followed, from the same principles, that the Establishment could not be a *part* of the Universal Church, except by being the whole, since it was in open warfare with all the rest. It could be defended only as a national institution, adapted to the religious wants and ideas of a particular people, and comprehensive enough to allow ample verge for their theological divergences. Any other estimate of its character was not only visionary and romantic, but suicidal, and must lead, at no distant day, to the dis-establishment with which they were already menaced. Its whole history proved that, in the judgment of the Church of England, heresy was nothing but the legitimate variety of religious opinion. He agreed, therefore, with Dr. Arnold, when that great ornament of their Church said of other religious communities, including the Church of Rome: "They are not all error, nor we all truth." But he agreed also with the Professor of Chaldee,—and this was another instance of the identity of their first principles,—in desiring to belong even to the "Universal Church;" provided only that Church was willing to reciprocate his cordiality, of which he did not at present see any immediate prospect. He approved free trade in religion as in everything else, but it could only be established by the consent of two contracting parties. His High-church friends might fancy that they belonged to the Universal—by which, he supposed, they meant the Catholic—Church, by virtue of an imaginary treaty composed in their own vestries, but that Church knew nothing of the visionary pact, and declined to deal with them on any terms whatever, except unquestioning submission. Her spiritual tariff was not subject to modification, and she was the only power on earth with which any sort of commercial treaty, founded on mutual concessions, was totally out of the range of possibilities. He could not but admire her "pluck," though he did not always approve the objects upon which it was expended, and especially her complete unconsciousness that she either was, or ever could be, "in danger." In this respect she differed notably from their own communion, as their present conference proved, and not in this respect only. If their Establishment had still to be called into being, the Catholic Church could not be more serenely oblivious of its existence. The Archbishop of Canterbury and the Bishop of London were no more Christian priests in the judgment of the Catholic Church—nor, he might certainly add, in their own—than the vergers in Westminster Abbey or the organist at St. Paul's. She created dioceses in this country, nominated her own bishops to them, and took no more account of the Establishment than of the followers of the late Mr. Irving, or the society of the New Jerusalem. She might be right or wrong in thus dealing with their National Church, a point on which opinions would differ, but the fact that she did so was beyond dispute. If, therefore, the Professor of Chaldee proposed to unite with them in defending the Church of England, a task in which they gladly welcomed him as an ally, he could only do so on the same grounds as himself, and must put away the agreeable delusion of belonging to the "Universal Church." No man could defend the Establishment, with any rational hope of success, except as an independent institution, complete in itself, wisely tolerant and comprehensive, and in which, at this day, as at all former periods, everybody was at liberty to differ, within certain undefined limits, from everybody else. They could not unite the generous latitude so dear to their own Church, and which was both its theological and its historical basis, with the

irksome restraints of a rigid dogmatic system.
The Catholic Church had chosen one alternative,
and they had chosen the other. Each had its
merits, but they could not co-exist. The free interpretation of scripture, to which they were
invited by their own formularies—and the free
interpretation of the Fathers, to which the High-
church party invited themselves,—could not be
made to combine with unity of religious thought.
The two things were mutually destructive, and
eternally incompatible. A uniform faith could only
be imposed by *authority*, and that authority their
Church had rejected for ever. Their dissensions,
therefore, were but the logical results of their
principles, and the Professor of Chaldee agreed
with Anglican Bishops of every school, and with
himself, if he might presume to say it, in regarding
such dissensions as perfectly consistent with the
healthy life of a true Christian Church. If he had
thought otherwise, or had deemed opposite creeds
inadmissible in the same communion, he must long
since have abandoned the Establishment of which
these were the most prominent and characteristic
features. Finally, there was yet another point in
which they were equally of one mind, for the eminent divine evidently believed with him, as his
whole career proved, that there was no spiritual
authority in the world which anybody was bound
to obey, unless it agreed with his own opinions,
and that it was the undoubted right of every

Christian to judge what he called the "Universal Church," and refuse to be judged by her. And thus they could easily combine together in defending the Establishment, since the great archaic principles in which they all concurred were infinitely more momentous than the accidental conclusions in which they differed.

ARCHDEACON SOFTLY thought it an advantage to have heard, in this prefatory discussion, the representatives of two such opposite poles of religious thought. But he could not agree with either of them in the view which they entertained of their unhappy divisions. He would not deny that, from the first hour of the glorious Reformation, doctrinal divergences had been freely tolerated in their communion, and in this fact he perceived no plausible motive for reproach; but at least they had hitherto been confined within comparatively narrow limits. It was only since the rise of the so-called "Catholic" school, that "our communion," as Dean Goulburn lately observed in his letter to the Vice-Chancellor of Oxford, "is becoming perfectly lawless." That school had repudiated the principles of the Reformation, held up the blessed Reformers to obloquy and contempt, and quenched the light of faith in a multitude of souls by reviving the superstitions and idolatries of the Papal Church. They were no longer what their fathers had been for three centuries. Hence the fatal divisions which now weakened their hands in defending their beloved Church from the assaults of dissent and unbelief. But disunion was not, as Prebendary Creedless wished them to think, a necessary fruit of Protestant principles. The proof was easy. No such internal conflicts disgraced other communities, which had been more faithful than their own to the pure Gospel as preached by the English Reformers. "The great Wesleyan community," as the Bishop of Manchester justly styled that evangelical body, always consistently Protestant, was a shining example to themselves, and, far from being agitated by intestine discord, visibly surpassed in religious peace and brotherly love the pretended unity of the Church of Rome. Let them return to the integrity of their Protestant profession, and they would recover the harmony which the Wesleyans had never lost.

ARCHDEACON TENNYSON saw nothing wonderful in the fact that Wesleyans, and other Protestant heretics, did not resemble themselves in fighting together about religion. They had reduced Christianity to such a very small number of doctrines that they had little to fight about. Men whose whole gospel was some miserable shibboleth of Calvin, Baxter, or Wesley, and whose religion consisted in eternally spouting about that, could easily contrive to agree together in their own particular nonsense. They had only to suppress the Sacraments, as these people had done, abolish all the mysteries of Revelation, and replace them by the practice of immersion, the Methodist craze of instantaneous conversion, or the Calvinistic tenet of absolute predestination, and there was not much left to quarrel about. When Christianity was dwarfed and stunted to such dimensions, the only possible topics of dissension, and he believed they were tolerably fruitful, were the tyranny of ignorant "elders," the presumption of illiterate "class-leaders," or the precarious tenure of a stipend which varied with the capricious humour of such plebeian paymasters. It was far otherwise with the disciples of the Primitive Church, and professors of Catholic theology. *They* had no higher duty than to defend against all enemies, domestic or foreign, the sacred deposit of the ancient faith. It was not permitted to them to sheathe the sword, as long as there was an adversary in the field. For his own part, he had fought with his bishop, he had fought with the press, and was now fighting with his congregation. He was ready to fight with anybody else in a good cause. Speaking metaphorically, fighting agreed with him. It sharpened his intellects, and gave a new zest to the truths which it was his privilege to maintain. Holy Scripture spoke eloquently of the armour of the Christian soldier, and he would keep his shield burnished, and his lance in rest, to deal with any modern Paynims who should cross his path. As for those within his own Church—bishops, clerks, or laymen, who wished to substitute the abominations of the pretended Reformation, which he agreed with Mr. Baring-Gould in considering "a miserable apostasy," for Catholic truth, he would fight them everywhere and always, in the valley and on the plain, by day or night, as long as he had a voice to speak or a hand to write. But he would defend the Church of England, in spite of the heresies tolerated within her, because she was the only pure branch of the Catholic Church in this realm—or, at least, though she had some present defects, they hoped one day to make her so.

Mr. Trumpington would cheerfully accept the unholy challenge of the Archdeacon, and contend with him in his Master's cause. He had been requested by earnest members of his flock to attend the conference, but had warned them not to expect any good from it, much less any benefit to vital religion. His brother Softly, if he might call him so in the bonds of Christian love,—(the Archdeacon did not seem to see things in that light, and made no responsive sign,)—had spoken stirring words of truth, for which he tendered him his thanks. It was because they were false to the great principles of Protestantism that their enemies were about to prevail against them. They had abandoned the ark of the Lord, and the Philistines had borne it away. They could only recover it by forsaking their idols, and turning, like the Israelites of old, in weeping, and fasting, and mourning, to that pure

and reformed faith which too many among them
had denied. They were reaping what they had
sown. Their divisions were the chastisement of
their sins, and they had become weak because
they had turned away from the Gospel of Paul to
the deceits of Elymas and the soothsayers of Rome.
Let Rome perish with her idols, but let the chosen
people of England gird up their loins, and follow
after the sainted martyrs who had left them a
goodly inheritance, and built up their Protestant
Church amid the fires of Smithfield. Sabbath
after Sabbath he addressed this exhortation to his
own people. There were some who now invited
them to cherish an adulterous love for the apostate
Church of Rome, and to admire her pretended
saints; but what had she ever produced which
could be compared with the great lights of Protestantism?
When he thought of the precious
Cecil, the apostolic Wesley, or the godly Simeon,
he was tempted to say, as Brutus said of Cæsar:

> "It is impossible that Rome
> Should ever breed thy fellow."

(This unexpected quotation from the play of
Julius Cæsar was attended with marked success,
though the company appeared to be variously
affected by it. For some moments it was doubtful
whether gloom or hilarity would predominate.
Archdeacon Tennyson whispered something to his
neighbour, who became convulsed with laughter.

Prebendary Smiles, after coughing twice impressively, directed a glance of just reproof towards the offenders, which they seemed to receive with complete indifference. The Rev. Silas Trumpington looked straight before him, or as nearly straight as an inveterate *strabismus* permitted, and appeared to glare at some object in the distance. The Bishop of Dorchester smiled, Archdeacon Softly sighed, Mr. Hooker seemed shocked, and Mr. Weasel took snuff.)

(After a silence of some moments,)

MR. HOOKER observed, with an air of extreme depression, that it would be very agreeable to himself, and probably to other members of the Conference, if the learned Canon Lightwood, who occupied so great a position in the Church and in the University, and who exerted so powerful an influence over the younger members of both, would state his views on the subject of their religious divisions. He should be glad to learn from one who could speak with so much authority, in what sense a community which allowed her bishops and clergy to teach the most opposite and contradictory doctrines could be considered "*the pillar and ground of the truth,*" which was St. Paul's definition of the true Church; and also, how far such a discharge of her dogmatic office impaired her qualification to "*teach all nations,*" which was the primary function of "*the Church of the Living God?*"

Canon Lightwood was not insensible to the extreme gravity of the questions just proposed. They had long occupied his own mind, and had been his greatest difficulty in dealing with the souls of others. He admitted that the time had come to look them in the face. The extreme divergency of religious thought displayed in that room, by men who were all equally authorised ministers of the same Church, and had all received the same commission to declare her message to the world, was only a too exact reflection of similar dissensions outside it. They might perhaps admit, in the spirit of Christian candour, that no community of professing Christians, from the first dawn of their holy religion, had ever presented such a spectacle of discord as their own. It was neither prudent nor manly to affect to ignore what was visible to the whole world. The rapid growth of unbelief, especially among men of cultivated intellect, was said to be mainly due to the conviction, forced upon our generation by the ceaseless disputes of Christians, that Christianity itself was a failure. That such divisions weakened the claim of their Church to be the teacher of the nation, and even imperilled her continued existence, no serious man would deny. But this, it appeared to him, was not the most serious aspect of the question. Other Churches had fallen, and their own might fall in its turn. If the floods should arise, and sweep away the ark in which they had hitherto found refuge, the catastrophe might be superficially explained by referring it to intestine quarrels, or discordant watchwords. No doubt the first tempest would be fatal to a ship of which the crew had no common language, and whose disorderly efforts only counteracted one another. If, at the height of the storm, the distracted mariners would pull the rudder in opposite directions at once, while each attempted to execute a private manœuvre which was probably the wrong one, and in any case could only succeed by the combined action of all, the fate of such a vessel could not be doubtful. But the true subject of inquiry in this crisis of their communion was not, he submitted, either the nature or the extent of the divisions which they all deplored, but rather their source and origin. Was it true, as Prebendary Creedless maintained, that they were the inevitable result of their principles? It was to this point that he would direct his observations.

That he totally dissented from the opinion of Archdeacon Softly and Mr. Trumpington, who referred all their spiritual calamities to the revival of Catholic doctrines, he need not say. The movement which they judged so unfavourably had no doubt brought into clearer view the fundamental dogmatic differences existing in their community, and in that sense had been for a time a disintegrating force. But he thought it must be admitted, with respect to those whom the Catholic revival had influenced, that it had conducted them to a substantial unity both of doctrine and ritual, and that it had done so by virtue of the *principles* which controlled it. Discarding the fatal privilege of private judgment (Dean Marmion was seen to smile), and its endless fluctuations of individual opinion, it had substituted for that eccentric guide the definite creeds and harmonious liturgies of the Primitive Church, the decisions of the early Councils, and the consentient teaching of the Christian Fathers. It recognised, therefore, an *authority*, virtually divine, which all were bound to obey, and made its decisions at once the rule of Christian faith and the test of human obedience. To call order out of chaos had been the aim of the earnest men by whom the revival had been directed, and he thought this object had been at least partially attained. He would say, therefore, as he was accustomed to say to those who did him the honour to consult him, that their present condition could only be attributed to the long suppression of Catholic teaching in their communion, and the almost universal oblivion of the most sacred Christian truths, such as the Power of the Keys, and the Sacrifice of the Altar. And as it was open to him to contend that the Church of England was no party to the heretical and subversive opinions which had sprung up within her fold, but had always professed, in spite of the perhaps unavoidable ambiguity of her formularies, to be framed upon the model of the Primitive Church, the origin of their shame and weakness was to be found, not in the Catholic principles upon which she was built, and which would have secured to her a stable and progressive life, but in their unhappy decay, and final rejection by a great majority of the English race. For this reason he could look their difficulties in the face without excessive alarm, and certainly without despair. He and his friends could endure their divisions because they hoped to overcome them. It might be said that it was only an experiment in which they were engaged, and that the chances of ultimate success were visionary and chimerical; but they would not relax their efforts at the bidding of pusillanimous fear, nor yield their hopes to the dictation of irreligious clamour.

(The Bishop of Dorchester bowed to Canon Lightwood with an approving smile. Archdeacon Tennyson glanced at Mr. Trumpington, who had closed his eyes, as if to exclude a too vivid ray of light. Mr. Hooker seemed more cheerful. Mr. Weasel looked amused, and again took snuff. Dean Marmion remained perfectly impassive, as if biding his time. Prebendary Smiles was radiant. The Bishop of Brighton frowned, half rose from his seat, and would evidently have broken silence, if he had not perceived that the Canon was about to continue his discourse.)

CANON LIGHTWOOD was far from supposing that

he had given a complete answer to the questions of Mr. Hooker, nor was it easy to do so. He admitted, with his friend the Professor of Chaldee, that defeat, not victory, might be at their gates. But he thought he had justified his own attitude towards the divisions in their community, and vindicated his personal belief 'that they were not necessarily fatal to its claims as a true branch of the Catholic Church. If the spread of Catholic truth should continue, they might one day be healed, when the objection founded upon them would disappear. (A by-stander might have fancied that at this moment Mr. Weasel winked at Dean Marmion, but would no doubt have rejected the supposition as too violently improbable.) What he had said thus far was an adequate reply to Archdeacon Softly, and other adversaries within their own communion, but not, he frankly confessed, to those outside it. He did not need to be reminded that the Church of England was not the only Christian community in the world. In addition to domestic foes, they had to sustain the assaults of men who belonged to older ecclesiastical organisations than their own, and whose arguments could neither be disposed of by an imprudent silence, nor refuted by the mere announcement of hopes, which, however legitimate, might never be realised. But even against such adversaries he thought they held a tenable position. It was certainly not open to the Eastern Church, for example, to reproach them with their disorders, since no region of Christendom was ever more deeply agitated by incurable and increasing schisms than that which professed the Greek or "orthodox" faith. The Russian was quite as purely a national Church as their own, and made no difficulty in avowing it. It did not even profess to be Catholic, nor wish to be. It had no voice for any people not of Greek or Sclavonic origin. It aimed at nothing higher than political unity. Moreover, it was undermined throughout its whole extent by sects constantly increasing in number—already amounting, he was informed, to a majority of the population—many of them of an odious character, and all animated by the most virulent animosity towards the official Church. It was a well-known prediction of the late Czar Nicholas, that "Russia would perish by her religious divisions," and they had enormously increased since his time. Nor could it be denied that Russian policy was provoking this dissolution of the empire, and courting the destruction of its Church, by directly fomenting schism in other lands. After persuading Greece to declare its complete independence of the Patriarch of Constantinople, the true head of the Oriental Church, Russia had lately induced Bulgaria to follow the same example. She was always ready to sacrifice religious to political unity, and only wished her subjects to be orthodox, in order that they might be Russian. A Church in such a state of growing disunion, and so completely subject to and enslaved by the civil power, was evidently not entitled to taunt their own with its religious divisions.

The Western Church, in communion with the see of Rome,—(Mr. Hooker appeared to listen with redoubled attention)—was no doubt in a less distracted state, and had found means to escape such calamities. He would not deny that she might boast, with an appearance of reason, that her members, of whatever nationality, were really united, not by a civil or political, but by a spiritual bond. Acknowledging a common centre of authority, which had a prescription of many centuries in its favour, and had come to be regarded by the largest body of Christians in the world as of divine origin, the lawlessness of individual and speculative opinion had been, it might be admitted, effectually restrained among the adherents of the Roman Church. She alone existed in all lands, and was the same in all. It was no doubt an honourable distinction, but though such unity of faith had been secured in the Roman Church, in spite of its diffusion among so many different races of men, it did not follow that the authority to whose action it was due was really what it claimed to be. He would illustrate his meaning by an example. The Greek and Indian philosophers of old, in spite of the errors of their astronomical system, and their total ignorance of the true motions of the earth, were approximately exact in their practical conclusions, and no serious confusion resulted, in determining the length of the year, and other problems intimately connected with human affairs, from the false assumptions of a blind and inaccurate science. In like manner, the unity of the Roman Church, which seemed to contrast so impressively with the chaos of other communities, might be produced by the exercise of an authority which was not really divine, but simply a human device or even a usurpation, and which had no claim to the obedience which it enforced, and had contrived to secure.

Mr. Hooker would venture to ask the learned Canon if he could point to any other example, in the whole history of man, in which a similar dogmatic unity had been obtained, and preserved for many centuries, by the action of a purely human authority?

Canon Lightwood did not know that he could.

Mr. Hooker might perhaps inquire further whether the same mysterious unity, which had been found so unattainable in all other communities, and especially in their own, had not been easily maintained even in England, during a series of ages, as long as the supremacy of the Roman Pontiff was admitted?

Canon Lightwood could not deny it, but it did not follow that the two facts bore to each other the relation of cause and effect, nor even, if they did, that unity *ought* to have been obtained by such means. He would presume also to warn his friend against attaching undue importance to a phenomenon which appealed to the imagination rather than to the reason. (Mr. Hooker appeared to relapse into profound melancholy.) He did not undervalue the blessings of unity, to which they ought all to aspire, nor dispute that, in a happier state of things, it had been represented, both by the Apostles and the Fathers, as an essential note of the true Church ; but he thought they were justified in accepting a disunion for which they were not responsible, rather than a jurisdiction which had never been acknowledged by the primitive Church. (Hear, hear, from the Bishop of Dorchester.) He knew that great saints had spoken eloquently of the "seamless robe of Christ," as an emblem of the undivided Church, but truth was better than unity, and if they must resign either one or the other, their choice could not be doubtful.

Mr. Hooker hoped his interruptions would be pardoned, but could not refrain from saying, that if Almighty God had made no provision to secure the unity of the Christian Church, it was difficult to resist the conclusion that that Church was not His work ; and if He had, it was a solemn duty to inquire what was its nature ? It seemed to him a suggestion both of reason and piety, that the authority which the Wisdom of God had established to maintain Christian unity must be *the only one which had ever succeeded in doing so.*

Canon Lightwood did not complain of interruptions, and respected the religious scruples which prompted them. He could easily understand that an earnest man might fix his thoughts so intensely upon the question of unity, which, he freely admitted, was a fundamental one, as to close his eyes to other and equally important considerations. Thus, it had been judiciously observed that Romanists laid so much stress upon the words, "*Thou art Peter, and upon this rock I will build my church,*" —"*to thee will I give the keys of the kingdom of heaven,*"—"*Feed my sheep,*"—and the like, as to suggest the suspicion that they did not value any other texts. For his own part, while admitting that whatever fell from the lips of our Blessed Lord should be reverently received and examined, and that such texts might seem *prima facie* to be opposed to Anglican views, he could admit no other interpretation of them than that adopted by the Fathers and early Councils.

Mr. Weasel: Whenever that interpretation could be made to agree with his own?

Canon Lightwood hoped Mr. Weasel would postpone his comments, which the Conference would no doubt be willing to hear, to a more convenient moment. He had been asked to state his own views, and was attempting to do so. That they did not coincide with those of Mr. Weasel was an inconvenience which he would endeavour to bear. The question actually before them was the doctrinal divisions in their own Church, the causes to which they must be referred, and their effect in paralysing their efforts to defend their community in its hour of danger. He had replied that the origin of their divisions was to be found in the growth of heretical principles,—that since they were at present unavoidable, their duty was to accept them with resignation,—and as to the best available methods of Church Defence, he should be happy to consider them, as soon as they approached a subject which these preliminary discussions had compelled them to defer.

Mr. HOOKER was grateful to the learned Canon for the patience with which he had received his interruptions, but could not say that his replies had afforded him much relief. It seemed to him, if he might say so, that Canon Lightwood confined his attention too exclusively to the *fact* of their divisions, and their probable source, while he said nothing of the grievous practical results which followed from them. Those results met them at every turn, not as unreal or speculative evils, but as a snare to the conscience, and a burden to the soul. His own Bishop, for example, holding perhaps the most important see in England, had publicly condemned the "Catholic Revival," from which alone Canon Lightwood anticipated any improvement in their condition, as "more disastrous than Puritanism," and had formally denied the doctrine of the Christian Sacrifice,—which he had been taught to regard as belonging to the very essence of their religion,—as inconsistent both with the Scriptures and with the formularies of the Anglican Church. No Catholic could doubt that this was deadly heresy, utterly subversive of the Gospel of Christ. Could he, then, without sin, remain in voluntary communion with such a Bishop? Was there any well-attested case in early ecclesiastical annals which would justify him in doing so?

CANON LIGHTWOOD was not prepared to cite a strictly parallel case.

THE BISHOP OF DORCHESTER must really say that their friend was over-sensitive. He was not responsible for the private opinions of those "set over him in the Lord." The liberty of judgment claimed by the Bishops, and always allowed by their Church, was equally the privilege of the clergy. In the present constitution of man such differences of opinion were inevitable. If their existence was a reproach, it must be imputed, not to their Church, but to the characteristic weakness of human nature. (Mr. Hooker did not appear to derive any comfort from this consideration.)

ARCHDEACON TENNYSON was thankful to say that he had nothing to do with Mr. Hooker's Bishop, and should not pay the slightest attention to him if he had. He found it difficult enough to get on with his own, and could only do so by setting him at defiance. Until the Bishops became more Catholic, he advised all true priests in their communion to do likewise.

The Bishop of Brighton was much edified, as he presumed the other members of the Conference would be, by the harmony, of which they had just seen so striking an example, between the professions of Ritualists and their practice. Canon Lightwood had spoken of an "authority" which all Christians were bound to obey, but he had been careful to put it so far back in a remote past, that there was no danger of its being a burden to any one in the present. Considering the resolute determination of a certain school to submit to nothing in heaven or on earth but their own will, this was no doubt a prudent arrangement. It allowed them to disclaim "the fatal privilege of private judgment," and then to make a more copious use of it than any sectaries whatever. He had always been struck with the extreme ingenuity of professing to submit to the "Primitive Church," as a pretext for submitting to nothing, and could not refuse a certain admiration to the lawlessness which preached obedience, and the pride which aped humility. Neither Dissenters nor Roman Catholics, he believed, ever spoke of the Bishops of the Church of England with such contemptuous irreverence as some of her own members. No

Church that had been seen on earth during the past thousand years was good enough for *them*. They reproved the Eastern, reviled the Western, and despised the Anglican Church. Yet he had no doubt that if they had lived in what they called the Primitive Church, they would have maintained just the same attitude towards it as they now did towards every other. They would have given as much trouble to the Bishops of the second or third century, as they now gave to himself and his Right Reverend colleagues. The same wilfulness and conceit which made them lawless and self-sufficing in one age would have made them so in any other. They were always talking about " the Fathers," as if they were their personal friends, and had lived only to prepare the way for themselves, but he was persuaded that if they had actually dwelt among them, they would have found that St. Cyril fell short in one point, and St. Athanasius exceeded in another,—that St. Jerome was unsound on this, and St. Augustine on that,—and would have been as forward to teach the ancient Church as they now were to teach their own. The only Church which these modest and diffident professors condescended to approve was a mere *nominis umbra*, which never had any real existence, and which they would not obey if it had. It was precisely because it was a creature of their imagination, too unsubstantial to cast even a shadow in their path, and powerless either to exact their obedience or chastise their revolt, that this ecclesiastical scarecrow received their pretended reverence, and dispensed them from an irksome submission to a living and speaking Church. Professing to obey what did not exist, they contrived to obey nothing, made themselves the sole arbiters of truth, and the only living oracle which could proclaim it. (Mr. Weasel leaned back in his chair with an expression of lively satisfaction, and even Dean Marmion, for the first time, appeared to be interested. Archdeacon Tennyson, also for the first time, became restless and gloomy.)

THE BISHOP OF DORCHESTER would ask his Right Reverend brother, whether they were to understand his severe language to apply indiscriminately to all members of the High Church party, and would request him to be good enough to tell them what authority was recognised by the members of his own?

THE BISHOP OF BRIGHTON had no difficulty in replying to either interrogation. As to the first, he believed that among High Churchmen there were two totally distinct classes, agreeing more or less in certain axioms and postulates, and in a rooted aversion to the Reformers and the work accomplished by them, but differing as widely in moral temper as any two classes of men in the world. He had little sympathy with either, believing them to be involved in a common delusion;

but he knew how to distinguish between sincere and modest men, affrighted by their religious divisions, and morbidly anxious to recover an impossible unity, and the petulant self-sufficiency of a meaner class, whose only conception of unity was that everybody should adopt *their* opinions, while they proved their respect for what they called the Catholic Church by asserting that it had ceased to exist in its purity for many ages, and that they alone were able to revive it. The first might obtain favour, and he believed they would, in the day of account, by reason of their humility; but the second appeared to him, and he would not shrink from saying it, the least modest or truthful professors who ever voluntarily repudiated their principles by their acts. Affecting to aspire to unity, their only contribution towards it was to add one more to the already existing divisions, by creating a totally new religion, which was neither Catholic nor Protestant; pretending to venerate the Catholic Church, they borrowed from it, like true eclectics, only what suited their own taste, while they rejected its claims with more deliberation than any sectaries whatever; professing scrupulous observance of Christian docility and ecclesiastical subordination, they recognised no authority on earth, not even that of their own Bishops, usurped every function which they chose to perform, and became a law to themselves. This was his answer to the first question of his Right Reverend friend, and with respect to the second, the only court of appeal before which he would plead was the Word of God; and the formularies of their own Church, so far as they were founded upon it. (Archdeacon Tennyson began to revive.) It was to that supreme authority, as they all knew, that their Church, in one of her articles of faith, referred her members.

CANON LIGHTWOOD wished to ask his Lordship, *who* was to interpret the Word of God, which certainly did not interpret itself, but commanded all men to "hear the Church," on pain of being numbered with the heathen?

THE BISHOP OF BRIGHTON feared that if the formidable menace were ever applied, the learned Canon would be one of its first victims. (General merriment. Mr. Hooker made an effort to smile, but failed.)

PREBENDARY CREEDLESS might perhaps be allowed to say, that for his part he would gladly comply with the precept in question, if any one would be good enough to tell him how he could do so? As no two existing Churches agreed together, and their own did not even agree with itself, it was so clearly impossible to "hear" them all, that a good many people had come to the rational conclusion to hear none.

THE BISHOP OF BRIGHTON was inclined to think that the precept was limited to the apostolic age, when the Church was actually in process of formation, under the guidance of inspired men, whose authority was indisputable, and therefore binding upon all. But this state of things was only transitory. As corruptions were gradually introduced into the Church, not only was her original authority impaired, but it would have been a sin to recognise it. At what precise period these corruptions attained such a baneful maturity as to release Christians from what had once been a religious obligation, he would not undertake to say.

ARCHDEACON TENNYSON supposed that, whatever date was adopted, from that time forth the divine command ceased to operate, and the Church ceased to be "the pillar and ground of truth?"

MR. WEASEL suggested that they might put it in this way,—that thenceforth Christians received, like convicts, a "ticket of leave," and were no longer subject to the annoying supervision of an ecclesiastical police.

THE BISHOP OF BRIGHTON would leave the Archdeacon to answer his own question. He would only observe, that whether the period was fixed two or three centuries earlier or later,— which was the only difference between his own view of the subject and that of the Archdeacon,— the result would be exactly the same. In either case, the authority of the universal Church was gone. If it were even postponed to the sixteenth century, the duty of obeying the so-called Catholic

Church was equally annulled, by the common consent of High and Low Churchmen. The Archdeacon was as much pledged to that view as himself. To say nothing of other corruptions rejected by those who founded their own Church, and emphatically stigmatised in her formularies, he would ask the Archdeacon whether the authority claimed for so many ages past by the Pope, and admitted for a thousand years by their own forefathers, was part of the Gospel of Christ, or a gross perversion of it? It was either one or the other. If the Pope was not the Vicar of Christ, as he pretended to be, he was a criminal usurper. If he was the first, the Archdeacon was bound to obey him; if the second, he must agree with him that the Roman Church, with which he claimed that his own was substantially identical, had ceased during a long series of ages to be "the pillar and ground of the truth." From that dilemma there was no escape.

Mr. Weasel: Except by saying, with Mr. Toots, that it was "of no consequence."

The Bishop of Brighton shook his head at Mr. Weasel, and continued. Or let them take the newly-defined dogma of Papal Infallibility. The Church which could make such a claim on behalf of her chief pontiff, profess to found it upon Holy Scripture, and affirm it by a solemn decree, was either the only representative of God in the world, or else the most reckless, depraved, and audacious impostor that ever mocked God and man. On the first supposition, the Archdeacon should hasten to offer his submission to the Roman Church; on the second, he must admit that she deserved, not the love and reverence which she still contrived to obtain from a majority of Christians, but the contempt and execration of all mankind. Which alternative would he adopt? Either was fatal to his own theory of the Church. If High Churchmen imprudently insisted upon a *literal* fulfilment of such promises as " Lo, I am with you all days;" " The gates of hell shall not prevail against thee;" " The Holy Spirit shall guide you into all truth;" and the like,—they must not only confess that they had never received any accomplishment in their own communion,—which began to exist in the sixteenth century, and had always allowed an infinite diversity of contradictory doctrinal opinions,— but that the Roman Church alone could urge even a plausible claim to be the heir of such promises. Either they were fulfilled in that Church, from which they affected to regard their own as the purest derivative, or they were never fulfilled at all. Such was the inevitable result of the suicidal theory of High Churchmen. But if the former was a conclusion which they found it impossible to accept, as their continued rejection of Roman claims and doctrines sufficiently proved, they must abandon all visionary and inconsistent notions about the immutable nature of the Church, which their own conduct disproved, and believe with him that the divine assurance of continual succour and permanent illumination was given to individual souls, and not to any organised society or corporation whatever. They must also admit that their religious divisions, which the Professor of Chaldee and Canon Lightwood concurred in tolerating, were simply the result of varying modes of spiritual apprehension, accidental peculiarities of mental structure, diversity of training and education, or different measures of religious zeal and devotion. In other words, they must put away all transcendental ideas about the unity or indefectibility of the Church, which were palpably refuted both by the past history of their own community and its actual condition, and be content to "work out their salvation," one by one, "with fear and trembling."

PREBENDARY SMILES (who possessed white and lustrous teeth, and seemed to rely a good deal upon the impression which they were likely to produce), hoped he might present a respectful protest against a view of Christianity which was equally fatal to the claims of every Church, and especially of their own.

THE BISHOP OF BRIGHTON would remind the reverend Prebendary that it was precisely the teaching of their own Church which most effectually confirmed that view, since she denied, both in her formularies and by her acts, that any Church possessed a monopoly of the truth; and when she added in her Articles that even of the Sees founded by Apostles *not one* had remained faithful to it, she evidently disclaimed such a monopoly for herself, and therefore consistently allowed her members either to affirm or deny, at their own pleasure, many of the gravest religious dogmas ever proposed to human belief. If the Christian Church was designed by its Founder to be always *one*, both in doctrine and discipline, then it was evidently the Church of England,—the most energetic living protest against that idea,—and not the Church of Rome, which was false, corrupt and abominable.

Canon Lightwood would respectfully inquire whether they were to see in such remarks his Lordship's contribution towards "Church Defence?"

The Bishop of Brighton had a deep conviction that men who desired to defend the Church of England in this moment of danger, and to perpetuate her existence as a national institution, could only do so with advantage by clearly recognizing her true character. They must first disencumber their minds of all the picturesque fables and sentimental theories which had found a place in theological literature during the last quarter of a century. If High Churchmen were willing to combine with them in a general scheme of Church Defence, he would not refuse, in spite of their extreme divergency of religious opinions, to accept their co-operation; but they would only damage the cause, and accelerate the catastrophe which they desired to avert, by affecting to regard the Establishment as part of an imaginary Catholic Church, against whose claims they were themselves in open revolt, or by disavowing the Protestant principles of which it had ever been the most uncompromising witness. If it could cease to be comprehensive, so as to represent the *whole nation*, with all its varieties of theological sentiment, or pretend to draw, like the Church of Rome, a hard-and-fast line of dogmatic truth, it would cease in the same hour to be established. It must continue to be what it had always been, or make way for something else. For his part, if he wished to demonstrate the essentially Protestant character of their community, and its constant respect for the claims of private judgment, he would not cite the unbroken array of bishops and divines, from Parker and Grindal to Sumner, Jackson, and Tait, about whose sentiments there was no dispute,— but rather those whom it was the fashion with Ritualists to claim, under the pressure of an exacting theory, as belonging to their own school. That some of them, in order more effectually to combat the Dissenters of their time, against whom they found it convenient to employ Catholic arguments, had occasionally used language which faintly resembled that of the more moderate High Churchmen of the present day, he would not deny; but the most emphatic declarations of sympathy with non-episcopal Protestant Churches, and the most unsparing denunciation of the Roman doctrines and practices recently adopted in many places of Anglican worship, were to be found precisely in the writings of those men,—such as Andrewes, Laud, Bramhall, and Bull,—who were now represented as favouring opinions which they abhorred, and would have visited with penalties in the ecclesiastical courts of their own age. If those departed worthies could now enter a modern Ritualistic church, they would express only surprise and indignation. But it was not necessary to go so far back in order to ascertain what was the true character of the Church of England, or of the capricious innovations by which it was vainly hoped to disguise it. They had only to suppose an Englishman, who should have spent the last twenty years of his life in one of the remote colonies of the empire, making his first appearance, on his return to his native land, in a fashionable Ritualistic church. Would such a man recognise, either in its novel doctrines or its unfamiliar ceremonies, the "Church of England" in which he had been baptised and confirmed, and which had taught him to glory in the name of Protestant? And when he began to converse with the clergy of this singular temple, and learned that the Church of his youth was "Protestant" no longer, but rejected the name as an insult and a reproach, that the

Reformation itself was "a miserable apostasy," and the reformers scoundrels and reprobates,—when he was invited to acquire the habit of going to confession, to assist at the "Early Celebration," in which he was to be careful to adore the consecrated elements, and found the ministrants clothed in sacrificial vestments, before an altar elaborately decorated,—who would refuse to compassionate the astonished stranger, or wonder if he asked what had become of his own Church, and where he was to look for it?

Mr. WEASEL thought it would be some consolation to the returned wanderer, that he would probably find it in the next street.

THE BISHOP OF BRIGHTON: Perhaps he would; but when he discovered, on further inquiry, that the new Church of England which had grown up during his absence had been created, not by the Anglican Bishops, but in spite of their ineffectual protests,—not by Parliament or Convocation,—but by a few enterprising gentlemen, some of whom had long since gone over to Rome, his perplexity would not be diminished. When he learned that the very clergymen who were its present advocates received their orders and their license from Bishops who utterly condemned, and would eject them if it were safe to do so, but with whom they remained nevertheless in contented communion, his surprise would be further aggravated. And as his means of observation extended, they would only tend more and more to confuse his mind. He would be told, for example, and expected to believe it, that the Church of England was *now* "the Church of St. Augustine;" and as he would probably know that Augustine was simply an agent and representative of the Pope of his day, and derived all his authority from him, he would hear, with evergrowing amazement, that nothing was more hateful to his clerical informants than those very pretensions of the Holy See which Augustine devoutly approved. Some of them would even tell him that this obnoxious Augustine was justly rebuked by certain British or Welsh Bishops, who were genuine Anglicans, and had a becoming abhorrence of the usurping See of Rome; upon which he would perhaps be tempted to observe, that if they descended from Augustine they ought to obey the Pope, and if they preferred a Welsh origin they must give up Augustine. They might make a choice, but they could not have both at once, as even this returned colonist, being a man of resources, would easily perceive. But still greater perplexities would be in store for him. When exhorted to go to confession, he might ask, but would get no answer, why so many generations of Anglicans had never thought of doing it? When invited to assist at the "Holy Sacrifice," he might, and probably would, inquire why the Church of England had utterly abolished it for three centuries, if it was really the chief act of

Christian worship? and further, if she was a pure and faithful Church for doing it *now*, what sort of a Church was she before she began to do it? and still further, if this was the holiest rite of religion, what must he think of living Bishops who declared, like the present Bishop of London, that it was utterly opposed both to Holy Scripture and the Prayer Book? In presence of these difficulties, and many more like them, he would perhaps begin to regret that he had ever left his colony, to come to a strange land, where everybody seemed to have lost his senses, and where he was in great danger of losing his own. He could only hope that he might not meet, as had happened to himself not long ago, a clergyman who would inform him that he was in the habit of giving "Extreme Unction" to the sick. Willing to humour this ornament of the new Church, which in this case appeared to be a good deal more Roman than Welsh, he asked him where he got the consecrated oil? to which he ingenuously replied, that he consecrated it himself. Inquiring in the next place if this was not, in ancient times, an exclusively episcopal function? he promptly answered, "that in case of necessity it could be done by a priest," and offered to produce authentic precedents, which he begged him not to think of doing. When finally he asked this lively theologian, why the Church of England had omitted to make any provision for this interesting rite, and hardly seemed even to have heard of it?—it was wholly unnecessary, was the ready answer, since she was a true branch of the Catholic Church, and therefore whatever the Catholic Church had done at any time, her clergy required no fresh authority to do now. He found this Anglican priest, as he called himself,—and who was quite right in saying that he did not "require any authority" for anything which he had resolved to do,—so extremely amusing, that he invited him to dinner, but had cause to regret his imprudent hospitality. After an hour or two, his guest's powers of entertainment were completely exhausted, and he became as wearisome as a parrot which could repeat only one phrase. But he had detained them too long, and would merely add, that he believed there had never been any form of religion in the world, in spite of the merits of some who professed it, in which logic, consistency, and common sense,—the facts of history and the precepts of reason,—were so completely set aside, as that to which he had been referring. The partial success which it had obtained among the educated classes was due to the revival of ideas and practices which had always a charm for certain minds, and gave satisfaction to wants which had perhaps been insufficiently supplied among themselves, but which were so evidently incongruous and out of place in their own communion, that they had been the main cause of the inveterate divisions which they were now vainly attempting to heal, and of the probable dissolution which they had too much reason to apprehend. The framers of the new Church of England were responsible for these results. He thought the true character of these gentlemen might be summed up as follows. They were so enamoured of *unity*, that they wished to keep it all to themselves, and would allow none to share it with them ; so devoted to *obedience*, that as they could find no Church worthy to claim it, they resolved to obey nothing ; and so submissive to *authority*, that in the absence of a living one in the present, they went back a thousand years to find a dead one in the past. Finally, while they refused to be called Protestants, they never cease to protest against everything on earth, and were so resolutely Catholic, that they communicated very little with their own Church, and not at all with any other.

(For some moments no one seemed disposed to continue the discussion. The Professor of Chaldee lifted his eyes to heaven, or would have done so, if the view had not been intercepted by nearer objects. The Bishop of Dorchester glanced at some notes which he had taken, but did not seem quite ready to use them. Prebendary Smiles displayed his teeth to much advantage. Archdeacon Softly endeavoured not to look triumphant, but with only imperfect success. Mr. Hooker was prostrated. At length,)

ARCHDEACON TENNYSON observed that he would

not attempt to answer the remarkable discourse which they had just heard. (Mr. Weasel seemed to think he had better not.) He would content himself with saying, that if their Church was what the Bishop described it to be, it was not worth defending, and their Conference was only a waste of time.

CANON LIGHTWOOD thought he had been so pointedly alluded to, that he might venture to claim their indulgence for a few moments. That there were apparent inconsistencies in the position of his own party in the Church of England, he would not dispute. No one was more conscious of them than himself. But he thought the Bishop hardly did justice, if he might say so, to the difficulties with which they had to contend. Those difficulties were not of their own making. They were taunted with being illogical, and violating their principles by their acts. They could bear that reproach with resignation. It was not their fault if Englishmen, carried away by the impure tide of Protestantism, had abandoned the faith of their fathers, or if many of their own predecessors in the Anglican ministry had done their best to assimilate their communion to the sects of Leyden, Zurich, and Geneva. The so-called Reformation, however excusable as a protest against certain errors of Romanism, had unfortunately conducted its agents to far worse excesses, and more fatal to true religion, than any which it professed to remedy.

It had destroyed unity, abolished authority, made heresy a virtue, and schism a jest. They found themselves, therefore, in this position—that while they could not accept all the claims of the Roman Church, they were still less able to approve the wild and criminal innovations of the reformers. In this difficulty, which they had no hand in creating, they turned to the ancient and undivided Church. They contended that whatever might have been the guilt of the actual founders of their community in its present form, they had been so far controlled by a merciful Providence as to leave a sufficient foothold for men who wished to be Catholic without being Roman. They were told, indeed, in a tone of bitter derision, that they made themselves judges of the Universal Church, and arbiters of all truth, and were thus guilty of the same crime with which they reproached Protestants.

ARCHDEACON SOFTLY was curious to know how they met the charge?

CANON LIGHTWOOD.—There was this clear distinction between them, that *they* acknowledged the divine authority of the Early Church, and wished to revive both its doctrine and its discipline.

ARCHDEACON SOFTLY: Did the learned Canon suppose that there was a Protestant in the world who would not make exactly the same profession with regard to the Church of the Apostles? (Mr. Hooker started as if he had received a sudden blow, and looked at Canon Lightwood with an expression of anxiety.)

CANON LIGHTWOOD (who for the first time appeared confused), would reply that Protestants, in making such a profession, were thinking only of a Church of their own imagination, which had never actually existed. They *could not*, without ceasing to be Protestants, have accepted the purely Catholic teaching of St. Peter and St. Paul, however loudly they might profess their readiness to do so; whereas he and his friends were prepared to yield an absolute submission to the Undivided Church.

MR. WEASEL: But only after deciding for themselves, in the true Protestant spirit, *what* it taught, and *when* it became divided. They admitted that the Catholic Church was *not* divided by the separation of Donatists, Arians, or Nestorians, who only formed, according to them, heretical, or schismatical sects. Why, then, he should like to know, was it divided by the separation of Greeks or Protestants?

CANON LIGHTWOOD (whose hesitation seemed to increase), could not admit that Mr. Weasel was entitled to interrogate him, in order to plead a cause which was not his own. (Mr. Hooker became almost haggard.) He would only say that such captious objections might increase the difficulty of their task in establishing the Catholicity of the Church of England, but could not change its nature, nor crush the hopes with which they would continue to prosecute it.

Mr. Hooker (who now spoke in a low and troubled voice,) thought that he at least was entitled to ask Canon Lightwood, whose counsels had once been precious to him, a question which merited a reply, and which he promised should be a final one. If he could not conscientiously communicate with the Church of Rome, because it proclaimed one or two precepts which he *believed* to be partial errors, how could he communicate with his own, which tolerated any number of what he *knew* to be mortal heresies? (This question appeared to produce a profound impression upon the company. All eyes were turned towards Canon Lightwood. After a few moments of visible embarrassment, and amid attentive silence,)

Canon Lightwood (who seemed to avoid Mr. Hooker's earnest gaze), said he had been reared in a University where logic was highly esteemed; but logic was not the only, nor the best guide, in questions of the soul.

Mr. Hooker (whose emotion seemed now to overpower him,) would ask what vestige of truth or sincerity could be found in such palpable evasions? No man could feed his soul with empty words, nor lull his conscience with the tinkling of bells. But he would trouble them no further. He was not ashamed to confess that he feared the judgments of God. He clung to no private theory, and would be the serf of no school or party. Truth alone was worthy of a Christian's love. If "without faith" it was "impossible to please God," he prayed for that true and living faith which was His best gift to man. If unity was a note of the true Church, it *must* exist somewhere, unless God had abandoned His own work, and delivered the world to 'darkness and chaos. If it was lawful to do in the Church of England what it had never been lawful to do in any other, there could be no clearer proof that she was only a human sect. From his youth he had diligently sought truth from those who seemed able to impart it, and now they could only tell him that no Church had taught it in its integrity for more than a thousand years. To be a heretic, they assured him, was a deadly crime, but to communicate every day with heretics was innocent and praiseworthy. To be an exile from Catholic unity might be a misfortune, but could not be a sin, and obedience was no longer a duty of Christians, because God had maintained no authority on earth which had a right to claim it. He had no ear for such impious lessons, and by God's grace would hearken to them no more.

(Mr. Hooker here left the room. That he was still present in the thoughts of the other members of the Conference was proved by a prolonged silence, broken only by occasional ejaculations.— "Beyond doubt a very worthy man," said Archdeacon Tennyson. "Sadly impulsive," simpered Prebendary Smiles." "A bitter fruit of our divisions," sighed Archdeacon Softly. "An honest fellow, and means what he says," growled Mr. Weasel. "Totally unregenerate," muttered Mr. Trumpington. Meanwhile, the subject of these comments was cooling his brow against a window in an adjoining room, to the extreme confusion of one of Dean Marmion's domestics, who hastened in an unreasoning panic to inform the butler, that "the gentleman was either praying or fainting, but he could not say which." On the arrival of that functionary to investigate so singular a phenomenon, it was discovered that Mr. Hooker was gone.)

THE BISHOP OF DORCHESTER (whose usually buoyant tone was somewhat subdued), regretted that a tender but too ardent spirit had prompted their friend to a hasty and injudicious withdrawal, which his more mature judgment would probably disapprove. It was no doubt sad that their intestine disorders, magnified by religious scrupulosity, should provoke a pious and earnest mind to a decision so precipitate and ill-advised, but when they suggested to a morbid and over-sensitive conscience that the only remedy for their religious divisions was the recognition of some central and supreme authority, to which the function of maintaining unity had been divinely committed, regret must give place to reproof. He believed they were at least unanimous on this point, however much they might differ on others, that they would never bow to such an authority (the Bishop of Brighton smiled); and as to the imprudent and groundless insinuation that God *must* have provided it, on the fanciful ground that there could be no true act of obedience where there was no power to claim it, he was sure the independent English mind would justly recoil from such a constrained and unreflecting submission.

PREBENDARY CREEDLESS thought the independent English mind was quite certain to come to that judicious conclusion.

THE BISHOP OF DORCHESTER (who seemed offended by the interruption, proceeded with increased dignity of manner). The Church of England was good enough for him, in spite of defects which time would remedy, as she had been good enough for Andrewes and Jeremy Taylor, for Wilson and Reginald Heber. It was one of her noblest titles to national esteem that she was discreetly, not unduly, comprehensive, and when she invited her members, whose liberty she wisely respected, to obey only the legitimate authority of an enlightened conscience, she proposed to them a higher and more generous form of submission than any ever devised by the ambition of pontiffs, or. the tyranny of kings. (Mr. Weasel shrugged his shoulders with contempt.) He did not agree with his brother of Brighton in disparaging the corporate and official action of the Church, and was deeply persuaded that the imperfections introduced into her fold by human infirmity, and the inevitable divergences of human belief, in no way impaired her claims to the respect of the nation, nor obscured her office as the great witness of pure and unadulterated Christianity to the whole English race. He need not add that he had no sympathy with idle and pernicious dreams of an ideal and visionary perfection of the Church, which were evidence only of an impatient and disordered mind, and were best rebuked by the spirit of moderation and contentment which he trusted would always animate the members of their own communion.

PREBENDARY CREEDLESS would venture to ask his Lordship, whether he desired them to accept such vague and colourless statements as an answer to the religious scruples of Mr. Hooker, or the incisive arguments of the Bishop of Brighton?

MR. WEASEL: No attempt had been made to answer them, except by Canon Lightwood, who had utterly failed. It was his decided conviction that no High Churchman *could* answer them, or would ever try to do so. Logic, they all confessed, was odious to them. He had long since perceived, and the present discussion afforded a fresh proof of it, that there were only two classes of men in the world, Catholics and Rationalists, who could reason consistently from their premises, or venture to accept the conclusions which flowed from them.

THE BISHOP OF DORCHESTER (with more warmth

of temper than might have been expected in a man of such elevated piety), would reply to Mr. Weasel, that he had not solicited his approval, and could contrive to dispense with it. (Mr. Weasel appeared to intimate, by an expressive gesture, that he would certainly have to do so.) Nothing could be more vexatious and unreasonable than to expect from the faithful members of the Church of England, who were content to use their own privileges in quietness of mind, a refutation of every delusive argument which a misdirected ingenuity could suggest. They were taunted by their enemies, and the taunt was re-echoed by some whom he would call false brethren, with their want of unity. The only pretext for this unmeaning reproach was the fact that they differed with respect to doctrines in which it was neither necessary, nor even possible, that all men should agree. It was a triumphant reply to such weak attacks, inspired by the insatiable malice of jealous and discontented rivals, that they all recited in the Church of England the same Creeds.

Mr. Weasel: How about the Athanasian, which two Archbishops, thousands of the clergy, and more than half the laity wished to remove from the Prayer Book?

Prebendary Creedless: And how about the manifold interpretations even of the Creeds which were nominally accepted?

The Bishop of Dorchester must confess with

shame that their Church was not what it should be, when such unseemly observations could be made by men who professed to belong to her communion.

DEAN MARMION would venture to suggest, that since such objections were urged every day by persons without their fold, they did not lose their gravity because they were repeated by persons within it.

THE BISHOP OF DORCHESTER (after glancing again at his notes, but apparently without finding anything to the purpose) was not ignorant that some of the worst enemies of the Church of England were men who ministered at her own altars, but only to deny her doctrines, and dishonour her name.

MR. WEASEL: Yet she was quite satisfied to retain them, and every private effort to remove them had always failed.

PREBENDARY CREEDLESS would remind the Conference of the historical fact, that Taylor, Tillotson, Hoadley, and Hampden, to say nothing of others, were all believed or known to be Arians, in spite of their subscription to the Creeds, just as one-third of the clergy were now Romanisers, though they professed to accept the Articles. Creeds and formularies had never prevented their bishops and clergy from believing just what they pleased, and no book or symbol, not even the Bible, could determine the faith of a community, as long as there was no authority to interpret it. The actual condition of the Church of England, whose members professed every thing, from Deism to Romanism, was a proof, and to his mind a welcome one, that in rejecting the authority of the Catholic Church at the Reformation, they had made it impossible ever to substitute a new one in its place.

THE PROFESSOR OF CHALDEE (who presented an aspect of contented misery) had not been more distressed by this painful discussion than he anticipated. But these melancholy revelations were nothing new. The Catholic-minded members of their communion could accept their cross without a murmur. There was no higher Christian duty than resignation. He prayed to be delivered from the restless and impetuous temper which made men discontented with their own Branch of the Church, because it was not all which they wished it to be. It was their own want of patient submission which was most likely to perpetuate the evils which they lamented. They did not deserve the restoration of unity, unless they could wait humbly for God's time. The winter would pass away, and for those who possessed their souls in meekness, and rejected the suggestions of discontent as a temptation of the evil one, a new spring would arise, when their Church would renew her youth, and be clothed with a garment of light. Meanwhile, it was their duty to share her trials and sorrows, instead of seeking in another communion the peace denied to them in their own. Providence would grant them not only the restoration of unity, but the full possession of Catholic truth, without any alloy of error, when they had learned to deserve those blessings. Let them wait. He had laboured for nearly half a century, in spite of calamities and contradictions, in the Church of England, and whatever others might do,—(here a solemn pause of some moments),—he would die in her.

Mr. Weasel had heard of martyrs of various sorts in times past, but it was reserved for the present age to produce a new variety, who were martyred by their own Church. He doubted whether the victims of Nero or Domitian ever displayed more serene patience under torture than their High Church friends. They would sincerely regret, he believed, to be delivered from miseries which it gave them such exquisite pleasure to endure. No wonder they refused to submit to the Catholic Church, when they could enjoy such sweet sorrow in their own. To live in a monotonous communion where everybody thought alike, where every dispute was promptly settled by a supreme and uncontested authority, and the Church was men's joy instead of their cross, would be to them an intolerable existence. They could not live without the luxury of "resignation." To believe only what their Church taught, and practise only what she approved, without being permitted to indulge in any private ventures of their own, would be a tame and insipid exchange for the delights of fighting with their own Bishops, superseding them in their dioceses, baffling the clumsy vengeance of the Privy Council, accusing half their brethren of heresy, and all the other palpitating sensations of their actual life. How could they endure the tedium of possessing Orders of which no one disputed the validity? Who could bear to hear confessions, as a mere ordinary duty, and with the sanction of ecclesiastical superiors, but without the charm of mystery, the delicious flavour of revolt, or the piquancy of self-will? What possible gratification could there be in offering a *true* "Sacrifice of the Mass," when authorised by a Bishop, and at which people only came to pray, compared with that of offering a fictitious one, in spite of the indignant Bishop, but which moved the audience to astonishment, exultation, or disgust? What enjoyment was there in a Creed which everybody admitted, or who would compare the dull possession of Unity with the rapturous amusement of pretending to search for it? What satisfaction could there be in belonging to a Church which had been monotonously Catholic for eighteen centuries, when they could remain in another which, after being Protestant for many generations, they were trying to make Catholic in their own? And then there was the entrancing doubt, full of delicious perplexity, whether after all it would prove to be

Catholic or Protestant,—a question which alone would afford inexhaustible entertainment to any reasonable man for a whole life-time. Who could be surprised if their High Church friends refused to part with such agreeable emotions, which they could enjoy nowhere else, or if they resolved, like the Professor of Chaldee, to die in a communion in which it was so extremely amusing to live?

He hoped that in making these observations he should not seem to be indifferent to the afflictions of his brethren. He was disposed to compassionate every real sorrow, but did not wish to offer an unmeaning and superfluous sympathy which nobody wanted, and nobody would consent to accept. He thought that when his High Church friends lamented their spiritual trials, while enjoying the varied excitements to which he had referred, they resembled a guest who should complain of hunger amid the profusion of a civic banquet. Their pathetic appeals to sympathy, and their profession of pious and placid resignation under their intolerable woes, should be sung in verse. Translated into the prose of common life they lost their savour, and degenerated into such droll confessions as the following. There was nothing in Christendom which they could obey except themselves, but they were meekly resigned to do it. They must sorrowfully dispense with unity, because there was nothing on earth at present with which they could conscientiously unite, but not a murmur should betray the poignant anguish of their souls. The Catholic Church was the object of their tenderest veneration, but it was their duty to revile it every day, and they could do it without shedding a tear. Their own Church was their heaviest cross, but they would carry it without repining to the grave. If ignorant Bishops, steeped in Protestantism, presumed to censure them, they would respond by calling their foolish accusers Successors of the Apostles, though they believed them in their hearts to be heirs of Simon Magus, and sons of perdition. If their fellow-clergy were unrepentant heretics, and impiously blasphemed the very truths which *they* proclaimed to be divine, they would remonstrate only by serving with them at the same altars, and thus generously defile their own souls with the very guilt which they shuddered to behold in others. Nothing could or should exhaust their "resignation." If all other communities wickedly laughed at their "Orders," and profanely scoffed at their "Priesthood," this should be to them only a fresh proof of the general corruption of Christendom, and of their own happy exemption from the common delusions of mankind. Finally, they were so sweetly resigned, and so enamoured of tribulation, that rather than submit to the only Church which taught all that they professed to believe, they would cheerfully remain in that which sanctioned all that they professed to abhor.

Animated by these admirable dispositions, he was not surprised that even the flagrant divisions which agitated their own body, though they surpassed in virulence anything ever witnessed in any other Christian community, should be an easy burden to *them.* Vainly was their indomitable patience assailed by so slight a temptation. They had proved that they could bear a good deal more than that, without any shock to their composure, or any perceptible diminution of their characteristic virtue. If a new school should arise in the Church of England, anxious to blend some of the more attractive features of Islamism with those of the Thirty-Nine Articles, he believed the proposal would find their High Church friends still nobly resigned. Whether the general substitution of mosques for parish churches would finally overcome their powers of submission, he had no means of judging; but if the Privy Council should decide, as it probably would, with a view to conciliate conflicting tastes, that they might be used alternatively, he did not doubt that their tranquil spirit of resignation would easily accept this inconsiderable addition to the number of "open questions."

ARCHDEACON SOFTLY must really protest against the light and ironical tone which the discussion was now assuming. He would not encourage nice and unprofitable speculations about dogmatic unity, and anticipated no advantage from foolish attempts to obtain it in their own communion, but he would remind Mr. Weasel that whatever diversities of opinion might exist among them, all sections of their Church agreed, as Mr. Gladstone lately observed in an eloquent and truly Christian speech, in " holding the Head." He trusted that if Mr. Weasel proposed to continue his observations, in which he had failed to detect any savour of spiritual wisdom, he would candidly give his attention to the impressive remark of the eminent statesman.

MR. WEASEL had heard the remark of the eminent statesman before, and was not much impressed by it. The fact—if it was a fact—seemed to him only a horrible aggravation of their doctrinal disputes. It was an amazement to him that any one could take any other view of it. If they did not all profess to adore the *same* Divine Teacher, it would be a comparatively small matter to attribute to Him a hundred contradictory precepts; but to affect to pay a common allegiance to the Author of revelation, while every one chose for himself, by the private interpretation of Scripture or of the Fathers, out of a mass of opposing doctrines, only those which his own judgment approved, and each insisted that *his* was the sole religion really taught by the Saviour or accepted by the Primitive Church, was perhaps a more impudent outrage upon the Master whom they all pretended to acknowledge, than if they openly rejected His teaching, or denied that He had made any revelation at all. To " hold the Head" was the very thing which such men did *not* do. It was easy to say that they only differed on " subordinate questions," but who gave them authority to call them subordinate? or what could surpass the impiety of applying such a name to truths revealed by God? It was not recorded, so far as he knew, that the Apostles ever classed the teachings of the Saviour under the heads of primary and secondary truths, or that they attributed to some an importance which they denied to others. All that fell from His lips was to *them* of equal gravity. They did not pretend to construct their own religion, choosing one precept and refusing another, but took it *all* from Him, who alone was able to teach it. To reject one iota of it, they understood, even while accepting all the rest, would be to deny His authority altogether. It would be to *teach Him*, instead of being taught by Him. And when it was considered what sort of doctrines were freely debated in their own communion, and every day indifferently affirmed or denied by the clergy, it was simply impossible to conceive religious dogmas of more transcendant import, or which could be less fitly described as "subordinate." If the questions which divided the High and Low Church camps were of secondary moment, he should like to know what were primary? There was hardly a point relating to either the nature of the Christian religion, or the constitution of the Christian Church, on which they did not differ hopelessly and fundamentally. It had been truly observed by an

American writer, that the disputes between a Baptist and a Presbyterian, an Independent and a Methodist, were utterly trivial, when compared with those which raged incessantly between High and Low Episcopalians. The latter differed on everything on which it was *possible* to differ. If one of these two sections of the same Church professed the religion of Christ, it was clear that the other totally denied it. Was it, for example, a "subordinate" question whether He had appointed priests in His Church, or only ministers? —whether the "Sacrifice of the Altar" was the most solemn mystery of His religion, or "a blasphemous fable?"—whether He was really present in the Eucharist, and therefore to be worshipped, or by no means really present, since He could not be "in two places at once," and was therefore "not to be lifted up or adored?"*—whether the Sacraments were intended by Him to be mystical channels of divine grace, or were purely symbolical and commemorative?—whether the unity of His Church was a law or an accident, and could exist at one time but not at another?—whether the Apostolical Succession was a fact or a fiction?—whether heresy was a crime or a virtue?—whether schism was a revolt or a privilege?—whether truth itself was one or manifold? And if, in addition to these domestic dissensions, on every precept of the Gos-

---

* Anglican Rubric.

pel and every mystery of religion, they considered further their fierce and cruel wranglings with that ancient Church which had been for so many ages the only Church in England, their pretence to "hold the Head" was still more shameless and indecent. Would any one dare to say, before men and angels, that the *Unity* of God's Church, or the provision which He had made to secure it, was a "subordinate" matter, about which it was lawful to differ? They might as well say that it was a subordinate matter whether there was a God or a Church at all. Was it a scholastic subtlety, a mere speculative fancy, whether the Pope was the Vicar of Christ, and successor of St. Peter, or a trumpery impostor?—whether the countless millions of all ages and nations, who had believed him to be the first, were fools or knaves?—whether the English and Russians, in recent times, who believed him to be the last, were obeying the ordinance of God, or trampling it under foot? Was such a chaotic jumble of nonsense and contradiction, more worthy of Hottentots or Ashantees than of Christians, the proper fruit of the Incarnation and Atonement? Was it for this that Christ died? Was this their boasted Christianity? No wonder that the very heathen, the Hindu and the Chinese, scorned such a religion, as soon as its self-appointed preachers appeared among them. And were they to be told, with a solemn mockery, as if religion were only a subject for jesting, that men who made such a caricature of God's revelation all "hold the Head?" If there was anything plain to reason and common sense, it was this—that if *any one* of the innumerable religions professed at the same moment in their own communion was divine, all the rest were human; and if the adherents of that one system, whichever it was, were servants of Christ, all the rest were in open rebellion against Him. They might pretend to "hold the Head," while they disputed about almost every truth which He came on earth to reveal, as if it was their business to instruct *Him* as to the meaning of His own words; but such Christians only resembled the *Frondeurs* of the time of Louis XIII., who all professed indeed to be royalists, but never ceased to wage war against the King, *in the King's name.*

Archdeacon Tennyson was not insensible to the eloquence and ingenuity of the speaker, who had certainly made some very striking observations, but wished to ask in what character he was addressing the Conference?

Mr. Weasel was examining the subject before them from his own point of view, and hoped the Archdeacon would allow him to continue to do so. He need not remind him that it was an inconvenience felt in every deliberative assembly that people were obliged to listen to opinions which were not their own. He thought it had now been sufficiently proved, by all which had been said during the present discussion, that the divisions which they professed to consider so grievous were, in fact, a very small burden to any body. It was a mark of good taste to deplore, but not in the least an obligation of conscience to remove them. Indeed, the only point on which they were all unanimous was this, that these divisions existed, and that they were quite sure to continue to do so. They would cease to rage only when the Church of England ceased to exist, and then they would reappear in some other form. The cause which produced them, and which existed in their own minds, being permanent, the effect would be permanent also. Only the action of a divine authority could produce unity, either material or spiritual, and the first principle of Protestantism was to make every man an authority to himself. It was sometimes made a reproach to the Crown, or to Parliament, that the free action of the National Church was unfairly limited, and the synodical deliberations of her clergy tyrannically restricted; but it seemed to him that the State could offer no greater service to the Church of England, no better evidence of its benevolent sympathy, than by mercifully prohibiting them from revealing to the world, that if they were all teachers of a divine religion, no two among them could agree together what it was. Without referring, which would perhaps be indiscreet, to the singular unity of opinions between their Lordships of Brighton and Dorchester, who both read the same Bible and were ornaments of the same Church, he might venture to observe of those less eminent dignities Archdeacon Softly and Canon Lightwood, that they proposed exactly opposite remedies for the malady which they agreed to lament. The one suggested, as a sure specific, to make the Establishment more Protestant; and the other, as a sovereign remedy, to make her more Catholic. He was afraid that under this treatment the recovery of the patient was doubtful. The first appeared to him a superfluous, and the second an impossible cure. To make a Church Catholic which had never been so before, was as if one should ask a crow to assume the plumage of a pheasant, or a dog to take the form of a horse. No such case, he believed, was recorded in natural history. Churches, like animals, must keep their own nature. Even the "hypothetical transmutations" of Mr. Darwin, prolonged through countless ages, could do nothing for *them*. A Church which had been Protestant in the first hour of its existence must remain Protestant to the end, though half its clergy should repudiate its origin, and learn to profess any number of Catholic doctrines. How clearly High Churchmen perceived this unwelcome fact was proved every day by their bitter hostility to the Catholic Church. Though draped in the very robes which they had pilfered from her sacristies, they ceased not to avow their aversion to her doctrine, and their contempt for her authority. Though professing to be quite as Catholic as herself, and even a trifle more so, and affecting the most enlarged and universal sympathies, a caged squirrel was not content with a narrower home, nor a mole with a more limited horizon, than they. It seemed impossible for them to be consistent for five minutes together. They were always peering over their neighbour's wall, and stealing whatever unripe fruit they could reach, though it was sure to disagree with them; but they could not refrain from pelting his unoffending servants whenever they came within view. Their instinct seemed to tell these imaginary Catholics, as soon as they saw a real one, that they were in presence of an enemy. It was a proof that men could not be Catholics and Protestants at the same time. They must take their choice. Cicero wrote admirable prose, but very poor poetry; and in like manner their High Church friends were excellent Protestants, though they did not seem to know it, but very indifferent Catholics. It was open to them to be either, or neither, but they could not be both. There was no such compound animal in nature as an ecclesiastical mermaid,— fish below, and *mulier formosa superne*. They must consent to be either all woman, or all fish. And even if they could attain, in some far distant age, the summit of their ambition, and leaven the whole English population, as Canón Lightwood proposed, with their own peculiar ideas,—a consummation which was about as likely as that all the fish in the sea should have the same number of scales, or all the birds in the air the same form of beak,—their failure would be only more conspicuous than ever; for their Church would still be, in the sight of all mankind, a purely local and national institution, as completely separated as in the days of Parker or Bancroft from the rest of Christendom, and not one hair's breadth nearer to Catholic unity. But if this would be its character even when their wildest hopes were accomplished, what must it be *now*?

(Prebendary Smiles here rose to speak, but was received with such evident marks of coldness, every one seeming to feel that any contest between him and Mr. Weasel would be an *impar congressus*, that after a prodigal display of his dental perfections,—to which he was supposed to owe all his success in life,—and a few weak phrases, to which no one paid any attention, and which need not be recorded here, he resumed his seat, but with the air of a man who felt that he had made his mark.)

PREBENDARY CREEDLESS did not wish to prolong a discussion which was evidently exhausted, but would ask permission to make a single remark. The whole question of their religious divisions appeared to him to lie in a nutshell. Either unity was an essential note of the True Church, or it was not. If it was, they did not possess it; if it was not, they did not require it. But on the first supposition, they did not belong to the True Church; and on the second, there was no True Church to which they *could* belong. Whichever alternative they adopted, the position of their High Church friends, whether in its religious or intellectual aspects, was not to be envied.

DEAN MARMION thought he rightly interpreted the feelings of the Conference in assuming that the question of their religious divisions had now been sufficiently discussed. It was true that they had come to no definite result, but this was not surprising. It was no more possible to arrive at a practical conclusion on such a subject, than to weigh a shadow, or dissect a dream. The clergy of the Church of England,—whose most solemn formularies were only a compromise between opposing doctrines, and neither affirmed nor were designed to affirm any definite theological system, except general antagonism to Rome,—had differed about almost every dogma of religion from the beginning, and would continue to differ to the end. It could not be otherwise. They might debate the subject for ever, but even if they agreed as to the cause of their dissensions, it was not permitted to them to agree as to their remedy. To search for it was as futile as to attempt to square the circle, or to discover the philosopher's stone. Religious variety was the result of their principles, and the law of their being. For his own part, he saw nothing to regret in it, for reasons which he would state presently; and he had the sanction of the most eminent living prelates, of both theological schools, for saying, that such discord, in the words of the Bishop of Winchester, was natural and inevitable. If they wished to be *one*, they must cease to be Protestants, and he presumed they were not prepared to purchase unity at that price. Every new movement in their Church had only revealed more clearly that doctrinal unity was for *them* a chimera. The history of the past did but confirm the experience of the present. They all knew what had been the issue of Laud's projects, aided as they were by the whole influence of the Crown. They ended in crushing disaster, and the Church which for a time they destroyed would never have lived again as a national institution, if it had not been politically associated with the restored monarchy, so that, as Macaulay observed, the Royalists "loved the Episcopal Church because she was the foe of their foes." In their own day, after a second total extinction of the most elementary Catholic ideas during a period of one hundred and sixty years, a new school, untaught by the past, had attempted once more to revive in the Church of England the "Catholic principles" which she was always rejecting; but though they had gained a temporary success far exceeding what had been obtained at any former time, they had only proved more clearly than ever that nothing in this

world could rise above its source, and that even in disavowing Protestantism, they remained Protestants in spite of themselves. In truth, modern High Churchmen had displayed, however unconsciously, a more intense spirit of self-assertion, a more complete independence of authority, than any other section of their community,—had created fresh barriers between the National Church and all other religious bodies,—and while professing, as their theory required, to aspire to unity, had made its attainment more impossible than ever, by proposing conditions which would never be fulfilled even in their own school, and could never be accepted by any other. They would neither admit, with Protestants, that unity need not exist, nor, with Romanists, that it had a fixed centre, and depended upon submission to an authority which all were bound to obey. Affecting to reverence the Catholic Church, against which their own was a living protest, they assailed it with more rancour than any Protestants whatever, and declared to its face, as every new sect had done in its turn, but with greater confidence than any :—
" We alone represent the Primitive Church, and we invite you to learn from *us*."

Every attempt on the part of Anglicans to restore dogmatic unity would end in the same way, and, as he had already said, he saw no reason to regret it. Differences of creed were not so much their misfortune as their privilege. The communities originated by the Reformation were all founded on the common principle that human reason—or the Bible interpreted by private judgment, which was the same thing—was as competent to deal with questions of the soul as with questions of art, history, or science. They denied that any authority had a right to impose on the human conscience a fixed and invariable faith. It was a saying of Kant that "philosophy possesses no axioms," and he thought the day was coming when it would be as generally admitted that religion has no dogmas. Its true sphere was the emotions, and its true function to form certain dispositions and moral habits, according to a type of which the New Testament exhibited the most perfect manifestation. He agreed, therefore, with Mr. Bain, that religious truth could not be imparted by any "intellectual medium," and that, " being an affair of the feelings, a method must be sought after to heighten the intensity of these." It was the boast of their Church, and he thought it was in some degree justified, to have formed in her members a certain spirit of temperance and sobriety, equally remote from the doctrinal enthusiasm of Rome, and the emotional fanaticism of Dissent. Her motto seemed to be that of Addison, when he spoke of "*Moderation* leading in religion" —as if to guard it from running into excess. (Archdeacon Tennyson and the Professor of Chaldee would have been at this moment an invaluable study to an artist anxious to depict the combined expression of disgust and consternation.) This was so evidently the genius of the Church of England, that the moment any attempt was made to commit her to a definite theology, its only effect was to let loose all the elements of disorder within her, and to create a general explosion. It was, therefore, with reason that the Bishop of Manchester had lately condemned, like so many of his colleagues, the principles of the so-called "Catholic revival," which, as his lordship observed, "are now a pure and simple anachronism" and "threaten to cleave the Church asunder." His own conviction, if he might say it, was this, that their discussion thus far had turned upon a wrong issue, and that before considering the nature of their divisions, it would have been more to the purpose to examine the nature of their Church. Upon this subject, therefore, he would ask permission to make a few observations.

The Christian Church was either a human institution, as he believed it to be, or a purely Divine organization, as Roman Catholics had always contended. If it was a product of man's wisdom, seeking to lodge certain spiritual truths in a more or less permanent home, not only was it liable to changes of form, like other human works, but subject in every age to all the tests which could be applied to it by the progress of thought, and the advance of science. In that view of its character, it could evidently claim neither fixity of form, nor perpetuity of creed. And if this was true even of the Primitive Church, while still contending for existence with the forces of Paganism, much more was it true of recent communities like their own, originated by the convulsion of the Sixteenth Century, and based on the private interpretation of Scripture, and the unhesitating assumption of the Nineteenth Article, that all the Churches of apostolic foundation, without exception, had "*erred in matters of faith.*" To fall away from the faith, according to this announcement of the Church of England, was the inevitable destiny even of Churches built, taught, and governed by Apostles. No member of the Anglican communion, High or Low, could venture, therefore, to assert that the Christian Church, or any part of it, was ever divinely indefectible in form, or exempt from error in doctrine, without professing in the same breath that his own, which ridiculed that idea, was a liar and a deceiver. For this reason he was not surprised that High Churchmen did not shrink from affirming, though to do so was destructive of their whole theory, that the Catholic Church had lost, for many ages past, both unity and purity—in other words, that they agreed with him in believing that she was simply *a human institution*. This was as evidently a first principle with Ritualists as with Quakers, Methodists, or Irvingites.

If, on the other hand, certain promises of the New Testament were to be taken *literally*, which seemed to him an inadmissible proposition, 'and Roman Catholics were right in contending, as they never ceased to do, that they had actually been fulfilled to the letter,—so that the Catholic Church had not failed for a single hour to maintain both unity of form and purity of doctrine, having been created by God for no other end,—it was still more clearly evident that of *such* a Church, their own, which began yesterday and might end to-morrow, and which permitted even to her clergy every variety of conflicting doctrine, was not so much as an attenuated part, or imperceptible fraction. It might be, and he believed it was, a valuable institution, adapted to their own age and country; but nothing could surpass the energy with which, in refusing to other churches, it consistently disclaimed for itself, all pretension to a supernatural character. The burden of such a pretence was more than it was either able or willing to bear. The Church of England was a creation of the civil power, for wise and good purposes, which, he was prepared to contend, it had substantially fulfilled. But the notion that such men as Cranmer and Barlow, whose private life would hardly bear investigation, Parker and Jewell, and their successors in the Anglican Episcopate, were, in any sense whatever, supernatural agents, employed by the Almighty to repair the defects of His erring Church, and endowed with special gifts for that purpose,—or that the community of which they were the authors and teachers was providentially exempt from those defects, and designed to be the indefectible substitute for a lapsed predecessor,—was the very delirium of absurdity, offensive to the conscience, and repugnant to common sense. They could not decently pretend that their own Church was divine, after she had taken so much pains to prove that every other was human. It was solely because the Anglican reformers asserted,—as Bancroft and Andrewes, Bull and Bramhall, asserted afterwards,—that no pure Church existed in the world, or had existed for a thousand years, that they were able to justify their own work. On any other supposition, they were themselves rebels and impostors. If they had imprudently admitted, instead of constantly denying, that the promises of Christ had been literally fulfilled, and that He had never ceased to guide, control, and inspire the very Church from which they separated, they would have been condemned out of their own mouths. This was acknowledged even by Ritualists, who strenuously contended at this hour, that the fundamental assumption of the reformers was just and true. They even adopted that assumption with more method and deliberation than all other Protestants. It was a necessity of their position to do so. If the reformers were not right in defying the Catholic Church *then*, they could not be right themselves in defying her *now*. If High Churchmen admitted, even as a conceivable hypothesis, or tenable theory, that the Church which converted this realm of England, and was for long ages the only teacher of the Gospel within it, had been for a single hour a *Divine* society, "the pillar and ground of the truth," the appointed teacher of the nations, and the light of the world,—they could neither justify the revolt against that Church in the sixteenth century, nor their own attitude towards her in this. Such an admission would be simply suicidal, and equivalent to the open avowal that they were themselves traitors to God and His Church. But they never ceased to justify both. It was, then, once more, the common conviction of High and Low Churchmen, that the Christian Church was *purely human.*

Such was the only view of the nature of the Church which any Anglican, of whatever school, could consistently hold. But he did not forget that there was another view of the subject, maintained in an older community than their own, and by a vastly greater number of professing Christians. It was the view of their own English ancestors for a thousand years. It deserved, even on Protestant principles, an attentive consideration; for if the doctrine of a Church so ancient in origin, and so wide in extent, deserved no respect, how much did their own deserve? (Mr. Trumpington groaned audibly.) He believed he was as free from prejudice as most men, and as willing to form a candid estimate of any system of religion or philosophy whatever, much more of one which had exerted a preponderating influence in promoting the civilization, and forming the character, of all the nations of Europe, including their own. He was, therefore, not tempted to deny that the Roman Church displayed an incontestible superiority over all others, not only in being able to point to her remarkable history in the past, and the priceless services which she had rendered to mankind, but still more to her astonishing vitality in the present. By whatever test that wonderful Church was tried, she seemed able to endure it triumphantly. If it was a question of *numbers*, her adherents had never been so numerous as at this hour; if of *doctrine*, she was teaching now all that she taught before the Reformation began; if of *unity*, a well-known German Protestant had lately observed, that her members, of every race and tongue, were " more absolutely of one mind than at any period since the Council of Nice ;" if of *authority*, no such prodigious example of its undiminished power had perhaps ever been witnessed, from the foundation of Christianity, as she had displayed since the Council of the Vatican. If anything might have been expected to break that authority by an intolerable strain, the recent definition of the infallibility of her chief Pontiff was certainly such an event ; yet its effect had been exactly the contrary, and not one of her thousand Bishops had refused to accept this amazing decree of his Church, though encouraged to do so by all the temporal princes, and almost all the organs of public opinion, in the civilized world. Even some who for a time had opposed it, and seemed resolved to do so to the end, had humbly obeyed that voice which never spoke with such authority as now, and against which resistance had never been so respectful and submissive. The handful of dissidents—a few German professors, and two or three French priests of little reputation—had totally failed to attract followers, though the forces of the world were all on their side, and had only added fresh lustre to the spiritual, by meanly soliciting the favour and protection of the secular authority. The Church which was able to do such things in this nineteenth century, by her own inherent power, and in one of the darkest periods of her political fortunes, was entitled to a respectful hearing, and would receive it from all but fools and fanatics. To men of independent thought she presented perhaps at this hour the most astonishing spectacle, the most inexplicable combination of political weakness and spiritual vigour, of which human reason had ever been invited to suggest a plausible explanation. It was a saying of Goethe, "When I see great effects, I am apt to suppose great causes," and it was the part of true philosophy to examine and unfold them. Nothing in the whole history of man was ever more worthy of thoughtful investigation. It was absolutely unique and unparalleled in the annals of the human race. For this marvellous unity of doctrine, and this continued action of a majestic and undisputed authority, were more conspicuous than ever in an age of universal doubt and restlessness, and in a world-wide community, wherein every form of mental activity was habitually displayed. It was, therefore, no light matter when such a Church, after an existence of eighteen centuries, calmly reiterated what she had said a thousand times before, that God had appointed a teacher whom the whole earth must obey, and then added, "I am that Teacher." For his own part, he was quite willing to admit, with some of the most advanced thinkers of the age, that if the first proposition was true, the second was true also. If the promises of Christ had been literally fulfilled, as the Roman Church contended, nothing was more evident than that they had been fulfilled in her alone. No other Christian community, ancient or modern, could so much as account for its own existence without asserting that they had *never* been fulfilled at all. She alone ventured to declare that they had, and that they would continue to be fulfilled in her to the end of time. And it was quite consistent with the almost incredible boldness of this assertion, that she never ceased, amid all the fluctuations of human affairs, to claim universal obedience, on the ground that she was not a human but a Divine Teacher, and that to rebel against her was to rebel against God, and to forfeit salvation. It was an imposing theory, as all must admit, and certainly if God had visited this world in order to make a revelation and found a Church, it was not an extravagant assumption that He had not abandoned the one to every chance interpretation, nor the other to every human caprice; but had established, for all time, an unerring interpreter of the first, and an undying ruler of the second. He would even admit that there was a certain plausibility in the doctrine that this was the only arrangement worthy of Himself, consistent with the general scheme of Redemption, or proportioned to the exigencies of a fallen and degraded race. He was purposely putting the case strongly, because he should presently avow his own firm resolution not to accept the claim to which he was referring. But he wished to state it fairly, not only on account of the source from which it proceeded, but in order to point out how utterly vain and unprofitable was the discussion in which they had been engaged. To waste life in talking about their religious divisions, which nobody expected to heal, was to imitate the shallow empiric whose diagnosis was limited to superficial symptoms, without even attempting to deal with the disease of which they were only an external indication. It was a mere solemn and pedantic trifling with a question which demanded quite other treatment. The only rational subject of inquiry for intelligent beings was, not whether this or that Church was nearest to the truth, which might be debated for ever, but whether *any* Church was able to teach it with authority. In that question every other was included. If there was no authority in the world representing God, and teaching in His name, their divisions were equally harmless and inevitable. On that supposition it was evident that the Author of Revelation was perfectly indifferent to the divisions which He had taken no means to prevent. But since the Roman Church was the only one which even claimed to be such an authority, or could offer the slightest evidence in support of the claim,—since she alone could point to an unbroken dogmatic unity, maintained through all ages,—either they must confess that they ought never to have revolted against her, or insist, as he was prepared to do, that there neither was, nor ever had been, any Church in the world which possessed infallible truth, or was able to impart it to others. That their own Church had any such power, or could unite her members in the profession of a common faith, was a preposterous hypothesis, disproved by notorious facts, and which, he supposed, no human being would have the hardihood to maintain. It was impossible to mix in society at the present day, without perceiving that the growing disposi to reject all authority, especially in religious questions, was due to the recoil of the English mind from the transparent imposture of a nominally Divine teacher approving totally opposite views of the same religion. Almost every day he met with persons, for the most part of cultivated minds, who assured him that they had ceased to believe in Christianity, solely in consequence of the attitude of the Church of England towards the fundamental contradictions of faith tolerated within her pale. His answer to such persons was, that this was precisely her greatest merit, and that since men must ever differ on subjects of such a nature, it was an immense advantage to England to possess a Church which distinctly recognised the fact, and even made it the basis of her claim to national support. Such a claim, he would frankly confess, was less repugnant to him than the assertion of the Church of Rome that the whole human race was in a state of pupillage, and incapable of arriving at truth without her guidance. She insisted, indeed, that her authority, far from suppressing liberty, only tended to secure it, by preserving men from the dominion of delusion and error, and that it secured it most effectually in that sphere in which it was most imperiously exerted. It might be so, but he preferred to obtain both truth and liberty by his own efforts, or to do without them. His mental constitution was impatient of shackles, and while he had a profound respect and admiration for the Catholic philosophy, and could not deny that it contrasted with their own in logical completeness, he could never consent to accept an infallible guide, or resign his independence of authority in matters of belief. Of course he was prepared to accept the responsibilities of that decision, and having to choose between order with submission, and chaos with liberty, he chose the latter, because it was the only choice which a member of the Church of England could make.

ARCHDEACON TENNYSON (who did not rise till it had become evident that no one else was disposed to do so), thought that in this lamentable Conference, of which he should never think without shame and confusion, all that was least lovely in their Church had been gathered into a focus, as if to present a grotesque and distorted image of it to the contempt and aversion of mankind. He had felt throughout the discussion as if wading through Milton's "Serbonian Bog," and was afraid he should bear the stains, and exhale the odour of it, to his last hour. A hundred times he had been tempted to think that he was a homeless wanderer, an exile from the family of God, or that, like Timon, he had

> " made his mansion
> Upon the beached verge of the salt flood,"

and that the next tide would carry it away. It was a matter for tears rather than for words. He would say no more: let others continue the discussion who had the heart to do so.

The Bishop of Dorchester would suggest that it was time to change the subject, and to consider, without further delay, what he apprehended was the main purpose of their Conference, the measures of Church Defence which they might think it expedient to adopt.

(No immediate reply was made to this invitation. A chill consciousness seemed to pervade the company that there was not much to defend. Every one looked at his neighbour, as if expecting from him the suggestion which he was not prepared to offer himself. Mr. Weasel put his hand before his face, apparently to conceal an irresistible temptation to laugh. Canon Lightwood seemed oppressed. Mr. Trumpington, without rising from his seat, said aloud, "Let us pray," and seemed about to do it, to the great alarm of every member of the Conference, but was stopped by the timely interposition of)

Prebendary Creedless, who observed that if the danger of the Church was great, and the desire to reduce her to the level of non-established communities openly avowed, even within the walls of the legislature, it seemed to him that she could not do better at this crisis than imitate the example of civil corporations which found themselves in a similar difficulty. The first attempt of every kingdom menaced by an external enemy was to fortify itself by prudent alliances. Was it not open to the Church of England to adopt the same course?

ARCHDEACON TENNYSON (who appeared to revive suddenly, and to have completely shaken off his previous gloom), thought it a happy suggestion. The Russian Church, he was sure, would gladly unite with them, especially if they could convince her, which might be easily done, that their own was not Protestant but Catholic.

DEAN MARMION feared that as she was not Catholic herself, and did not profess to be, the proof of their own Catholicity, whenever it was forthcoming, would not avail much. The Holy Synod might affect to entertain proposals of alliance, with the permission of the Czar, and be quite willing that individual Episcopalians should pay compliments to the "Orthodox" Church, as they had lately done in New York, but there was about as much chance of union with the Church of Russia as with the Church in the Moon, if any such community existed. And even if the union could be accomplished, since it was only desired by a portion of their own members, and would be odious to all the rest, it could but intensify their existing divisions, and afford one more proof to the world how utterly indifferent the Church of England was to dogmatic unity. Moreover, the Roman doctrine of devotion to the "Mother of God," which was more offensive to Englishmen than any other, was actually exaggerated in the "Orthodox" Church, and constituted in fact, together with the *cultus* of a few doubtful Russian saints, almost the whole religion of the Russian people.

ARCHDEACON TENNYSON was quite willing, for his part, to unite with the Church of Rome (Mr. Trumpington hastily left the room, and was seen no more), provided she would confess that their own was as true a Church as herself.

ARCHDEACON SOFTLY thought that a proposal to re-unite with the Church of Rome was equivalent to a confession that they ought never to have separated from her. But it was some consolation to know that such a proposal, if it should ever be seriously made, which did not seem to him probable, would certainly be declined. If he was rightly informed, the authorities of the Roman Church had not long ago announced that it would not even be entertained, and that Anglicans could only be received into her communion one by one, after renouncing their errors, and submitting themselves without reserve to her supreme authority. He was sincerely glad to hear it, and hoped it would operate as a timely check to any unprofitable movement in that direction. For his own part, he was disposed to look for allies in a very different quarter. It was among their own countrymen, professing the pure doctrines of the Reformation, that he would seek Christian sympathy and co-operation. The Bishop of Manchester had observed, in his primary Charge, that "the great Wesleyan community had not yet shown any disposition to join in the attack upon the Church," and that since they professed the same faith with themselves, and were "superior to them in discipline," their adhesion to the National Church would be "as life from the dead." He cordially sympathised with that opinion, and trusted that overtures would be made in a spirit of conciliation to secure so joyful a result.

PREBENDARY CREEDLESS was afraid that an alliance with Wesleyans was as wild a speculation as a union with the Holy Synod or the Vatican. He had seen lately what appeared to be an official statement on the part of that "great community," which certainly did not encourage the idea that they were likely to accept the amiable invitation of the Archdeacon.

THE BISHOP OF DORCHESTER begged to observe that no such invitation had been addressed, or was likely to be addressed, to the Wesleyans by any one having authority to do so.

MR. WEASEL (who seemed to find particular satisfaction in contradicting the Bishop of Dorchester), would reply, that such an invitation had actually been given by an eminent dignitary of their Church, and in very impressive terms. He did not concur with his learned friend in the step which he had taken, but supposed that he wished to inject Methodism into the veins of the Establishment, on the principle that certain poisons became curative in morbid states of the body. As the catalogue of possible alliances appeared exhausted, and they would evidently have to fight their battles alone, without the aid of auxiliaries of any creed whatever, he might perhaps venture to offer a suggestion. Was it not open to them to imitate the peaceful policy of the Government, and submit the future existence of the Establishment to *arbitration?* He presumed that the President of the Wesleyan Conference, the Moderator of the Free Kirk, and, say, Dr. Döllinger, would willingly undertake to decide whether the Church of England ought to be allowed to exist any longer, and, if they decided in the affirmative, would kindly suggest a *modus vivendi.* (Archdeacon Tennyson, yielding to a movement of indignation, quitted the room.) He really thought this might be a better way of settling the question than to provoke acrimonious debates in Parliament, with the certainty that the Government would throw the Establishment overboard as soon as the interests of their party required the sacrifice. The nation had already gained so much by arbitration, that the application of the principle in this case would no doubt be attended with cheerful results.

(The suggestion of Mr. Weasel did not appear to excite enthusiasm. The only response was a dismal silence, and the Conference presented generally a nerveless and debilitated aspect. No one seemed to have anything to say, or any wish to say it. The Professor of Chaldee walked slowly away, still wearing an expression of perfectly resigned misery, and seemed to utter a meek and silent protest against everything in general. Canon Lightwood followed him. The Bishop of Dorchester inquired if his carriage was ready, and departed with so much precipitancy that he forgot to salute the company. Prebendary Smiles appeared to glide from the room, omitting even to display his teeth, perhaps because it was hardly worth while to show them to so few spectators. One by one the members of the Conference disappeared, till only Mr. Weasel and Dean Marmion were left. For some moments they looked intently at each other, with a singular expression, which it would be difficult to interpret, but which seemed to indicate suppressed mirth. At length both exploded simultaneously in a burst of laughter, Mr. Weasel leaning against a table, and the Dean throwing himself into an easy-chair. When they had partly recovered, the following familiar dialogue ensued.)

"My dear Marmion," said Mr. Weasel, wiping the tears from his eyes, "how could you invite those fellows to come here and make fools of themselves?"

"Pardon me," replied the Dean, who was still

catching his breath, and seemed to have some difficulty in doing it; "I had no such purpose. I wanted to show that there was at least one thing in which we could co-operate, and really believed it. It is not my fault if my good intentions have been frustrated. How could I tell that they would all quarrel together, like the Greeks when the Saracens were knocking at their doors, and refuse to unite even *pro aris et focis?* Besides, it was chiefly your doing. If I had imagined that you could make such an indiscreet speech, I would not have invited you." (Mr. Weasel seemed to think this an excellent joke.) "They could endure the Bishop of Brighton, who displayed more capacity than I thought he possessed, because they are accustomed to that sort of thing, and don't mind it; but your abominable satire was too much for them. As soon as you sat down, I saw there was an end of the Conference. I really believe you have more sympathy with Hooker than with any of the others, and that your secret intellectual leanings are towards Popery."

"I hardly know what they are myself," responded Mr. Weasel; "but they are certainly not towards the Church of England. I remember that some years ago poor Thackeray, who had a low opinion of his fellow creatures, and not a high one of the Anglican Church, went with a Roman Catholic friend to a service at the Oratory. When they came out, his friend asked what he thought of it. 'There are only two realities in the world,' replied Thackeray, ' Rome and Babylon. For the present I belong to Babylon.' I fancy that is about my own position, and the more I see of my reverend brethren, including yourself, the more I am confirmed in it. What was the τέλος of your own speech but this, that if the Roman is not the Church of God, there never was one? You choose the latter alternative, and therefore you are a Babylonian. As to those fellows who were here just now, it is hard to say what they are. Tennyson has fine qualities, but he is the victim of one idea, and is no more capable of adding another to it than that noodle Trumpington. Give him plenty of room to fight in, and something to fight about, and he would not leave the Church of England though the Archangel Michael' implored him to do so. Lightwood is harder to understand. He is really a man of talent, a sound scholar, and apparently conscientious; yet, as Hooker easily detected, he abdicates reason altogether when it is a question of the Church of England, and resembles a mathematician who should admit all the postulates of his science, but deny all its conclusions. As to his Lordship of Dorchester, I believe he has no more true religion, of any kind, than a hedge-stake, and when he said the Church of England was 'good enough for him,' he only did himself justice. But really there must be truth *somewhere*, unless the God of Christians is like Baal, 'asleep or on a journey,' which does not seem probable. If He raised up such a spiritual colossus as Elijah, and many more like him, to be a light to the people of Israel, can it be supposed that He has abandoned Christians to such pitiful guides as Smiles or Dorchester, such stammering prophets as Lightwood or the Professor of Chaldee? Was the Law more glorious than the Gospel, and the Church of the Patriarchs more noble than that of Jesus Christ? None but a Jew could believe it. 'No,' answers the Roman Church, 'He still produces in *me* supernatural men, of the school of Elijah and St. Paul.' 'Yes,' replies Dean Marmion, 'we are all human now, and our Church is as feeble as ourselves.' It may be so, but in that case it is clear, as Thackeray said, that the only choice is between Rome and Babylon. All thinking men are coming to that conclusion. Philosophers admit, men of science proclaim it. I am convinced that the Church of England is responsible for this state of things. People see plainly enough that *she* is only human, and therefore conclude that nothing is divine. But if this must be admitted, 'Motley's the only wear,' as Jaques says, and Christians must fall back on the old pagan maxim: 'Let us eat and drink, for to-morrow we die.'".

"My dear Weasel," said Dean Marmion, "I never saw you in such a mood. My Lord of Dorchester has been too much for your nerves. I confess he is trying, but who is not? If you want authority, certainty, unity, the supernatural, and all that sort of thing, you know where to find them. My own tastes do not incline in that direction. The Church of England will probably last my time, and if, as Metternich said, *après moi le déluge*, there is something to be done meanwhile. We can fight against all shams and impostures, be content to pass for what we really are, and contend for logic against Lightwood, for religion against Dorchester, and for common sense against Trumpington. Fighting agrees with me, as Tennyson said, only I must choose my own weapons, and use them after my own manner."

Here the friends shook hands and parted. Any one who had followed Mr. Weasel, as he walked slowly down the street, might have heard him give forth to the night air, with a melancholy smile, these two lines of the poet—.

"'Charge, Chester, charge! on, Stanley, on!' Were the last words of Marmion."

THE END.

R. WASHBOURNE, 18, PATERNOSTER ROW LONDON.

R. WASHBOURNE'S CATALOGUE OF BOOKS,

18 PATERNOSTER ROW, LONDON.

10 ———— '78

NEW BOOKS.

Inner Life of Pere Lacordaire, O.P. From the French, by the author of "The Knights of St. John." New edition, revised, 6s. 6d.

Life of the Venerable Elizabeth Canori Mora. Translated from the Italian, with Preface by Lady Herbert. With Photograph, 3s. 6d.

Lives of the Early Popes. St. Peter to St. Silvester. By Rev. Thomas Meyrick, M.A. 8vo.

Tales of the Jewish Church. By Charles Walker. 12mo., 2s. 6d.

The Duties of Christian Parents. Conferences by Père Matignon. Translated by Lady Constance Bellingham, with Preface by Mgr. Capel, 12mo., 5s. *In the Press.*

Short Meditations, for every day in the Year. By an anonymous Italian author. Translated by Dom Edmund J. Luck, O.S.B. Prefaced by a letter of recommendation from His Eminence Cardinal Manning, 12mo. Edition for the Regular Clergy, 2 vols., 9s. Edition for the Secular Clergy, 2 vols., 9s.

Fr. Power's Catechism: Doctrinal, Moral, Historical, and Liturgical. Fourth Edition, enlarged, 3 vols., 10s. 6d.

The Rejection of Catholic Doctrines, attributable to the Non-Realization of Primary Truths. Exemplified in Letters to a Friend on Devotion to the B.V.M., the Angels, and Saints. By a Layman, 8vo., 1s.

On what Authority do I accept Christianity? A Question for reasonable Members of the Church of England. 12mo., 6d.

Manual of Sacred Chant, containing the Ordinary of the Mass, the Psalms and Hymns of Vespers and Compline, &c., &c. Music and Words. By Rev. J. Mohr, S.J., 18mo., 2s. 6d.

Cantiones Sacrae. A Collection of Hymns and Devotional Chants for the different Seasons of the Year, &c., &c. Music and Words. By Rev. J. Mohr, S.J., 8vo., 5s.

*** *Though this Catalogue does not contain many of the books of other Publishers, R. W. can supply any, no matter by whom they are published. All orders, so far as possible, will be executed the same day.*

School Books, *with the usual reduction,* Copy Books, and other Stationery, Rosaries, Medals, Crucifixes, Scapulars, Incense, Candlesticks, Vases, &c., &c., supplied.

Foreign Books supplied. The publications of the leading Publishers kept in stock. R. Washbourne's Catalogue of Books published in America, post free.

Life of the Rt. Rev. Dr. Dixon, Primate of all Ireland. By Sister M. F. Clare. 8vo., 7s. 6d.

Manuel de Conversation. 12mo., 1s.

Allah Akbar—God is Great. An Arab Legend of the Siege and Conquest of Granada. From the Spanish. By Mariana Monteiro. Contents :—1. The Genius of the Alhambra. 2. The King Abu-Abd-Allah el Zogirbi. 3. Zegries and Abencerrajes. 4. The Cypress of the Sultana. 5. The Chamber of Lions. 6. The Judgment of God. 7. Hernan Perez del Pulgar. 8. The Triumph of the Ave Maria. 9. Gonzalo Fernandez de Cordova. 10. The Conquest of Granada. 11. The Last Adieu.
Illustrated with Head Pieces from the pencil of Miss Henriqueta Monteiro, and elaborately bound in accordance with the Arabic. 8vo., 3s. 6d.

The Fairy Ching; or the Chinese Fairies' Visit to England. By Henrica Frederic. 12mo., cloth extra, 1s., gilt edges, 1s. 6d.

What Catholics do not Believe. By the Right Rev. Bishop Ryan, Coadjutor to the Archbishop of St. Louis. 12mo., 1s.

Life of Fr. Benvenuto Bambozzi, O.M.C., of the Conventual Friars Minor. Translated from the Italian (2nd Edition) of Fr. Nicholas Treggiari, D.D. 12mo., 5s. *In the Press.*

OREMUS, A Liturgical Prayer Book: with the Imprimatur of the Cardinal Archbishop of Westminster. An adaptation of the Church Offices: containing Morning and Evening Devotions; Devotion for Mass, Confession, and Communion, and various other Devotions; Common and Proper, Hymns, Lessons, Collects, Epistles and Gospels for Sundays, Feasts, and Week Days; and short notices of over 200 Saints' Days. Also short Liturgical Devotions for Holy Week. For greater convenience, the Latin has been given of all the Psalms, Hymns, and other Prayers, occurring in the ordinary services of the Church, in which the Faithful take more or less part. 32mo., 452 pages, paper cover, 2s.; cloth, 2s. 6d.; embossed, red edges, 3s. 6d.; French morocco, 4s. 6d.; calf, 5s. 6d.; morocco, 6s.; Russia, 8s. 6d. Also in superior or more expensive bindings.

Are You Safe in the Church of England? A Question for Anxious Ritualists. By an Ex-Member of the Congregation of S. Bartholomew, Brighton [Charles Walker]. 8vo., 6d.

Practical Hints on the Education of the Sons of Gentlemen. By an Educator. 8vo., 1s. Contents :—1. Introduction. 2. The Mind. 3. Preparatory Education. 4. The Existing System of Education. 5. How to Manage a Class. 6. The Educator. 7. A Plea for the Study of Language.

The Child of Mary's Manual. Compiled from the French. Second Edition, with the Imprimatur of the Bishop of Clifton. 1s.

Gathered Gems from Spanish Authors. By Mariana Monteiro, author of "The Monk of the Monastery of Yuste." 3s.

Life of St. Wenefred, Virgin Martyr and Abbess, Patroness of North Wales and Shrewsbury. By Rev. T. Meyrick, M.A. 2s.

R. Washbourne, 18 *Paternoster Row London.*

A Catechism for First Confession. By the Rev. R. G. Davis. *Nihil Obstat:* Johannes Can. Crookall, S.T.D.,V.G. 32mo., 1d.
Stories of the Saints. By M. F. S. Saints of the Early Church. 12mo., 4th Series, 3s. 6d.; 5th Series, 3s. 6d.
The Holy Mass: The Sacrifice for the Living and the Dead. By Rev. M. Müller, C.SS.R. 12mo., 10s. 6d.
The Faith of our Fathers: Being a Plain Exposition and Vindication of the Church founded by our Lord Jesus Christ. By Most Rev. Archbishop Gibbons, 12mo. 4s.; paper covers, 2s. nett.

ADELSTAN (Countess), Sketch of her Life and Letters, From the French of the Rev. Père Marquigny, S.J. 1s. & 2s. 6d.
Adolphus; or, the Good Son. 18mo., 6d.
Adventures of a Protestant in Search of a Religior. By Iota. 12mo., 2s. and 3s. 6d.
AGNEW (Mme.), Convent Prize Book. 12mo., 3s. 6d.
A'KEMPIS—Following of Christ. Pocket Edition, 32mo., 1s.; embossed red edges, 1s. 6d.; roan, 2s.; French morocco, 2s. 6d.; calf or morocco, 4s. 6d.; gilt, 5s. 6d.; russia, with clasp, &c., 10s. 6d.; ivory, with rims and clasp, 15s., 16s., 18s.; morocco antique, with corners and clasps, 17s. 6d.; russia, ditto, ditto, 16s., 20s.
——— **Imitation of Christ; with Reflections.** 32mo., 1s.; Persian calf, 3s. 6d.; 12mo., 3s. 6d.; mor., 10s. 6d.; mor. ant. 25s.
——— **The Three Tabernacles.** 16mo., 2s. 6d.
Albertus Magnus. *See* Dixon (Rev. Fr. T. A.).
Album of Christian Art. Twenty-three original composition Professor Klein, in Vienna. 4to., 7s. 6d.
Allah Akbar—God is Great. An Arab Legend of the Siege and Conquest of Granada. From the Spanish. By Mariana Monteiro. 12mo., 3s. 6d.
ALLIES (T. W.), St. Peter; his Name and his Office. 5s.
Alphabet of Scripture Subjects. On a large sheet, 1s.; coloured, 2s., mounted to fold in a book, 3s. 6d.
ALZOG'S Universal Church History. 8vo., Vols. i & ii, each 20s.
AMHERST (Rt. Rev. Dr.), Lenten Thoughts. 2s. 6d.
ANDERDON (Rev. W. H., S.J.), To Rome and Back. Fly-Leaves from a Flying Tour. 12mo., 2s.
ANDERSEN (Carl), Three Sketches of Life in Iceland. Translated by Myfanwy Fenton. 12mo., 2s. 6d.
Angela Merici (S.) Her Life, her Virtues, and her Institute. From the French of the Abbé G. Becterné. 12mo., 4s. 6d.
Angela's (S.) Manual: a Book of Devout Prayers and Exercises for Female Youth. 2s.; Persian, 3s. 6d.; calf, 4s. 6d.
Angels (The) and the Sacraments. 16mo., 1s.
——— **Month of the Holy Angels.** By Abbé Ricard. 1s.
Angelus (The). A Monthly Magazine. 8vo., 1d. Yearly subscription, post free, 1s. 6d. Volume for 1876, cloth, 2s. 6d. 1877, 2s.
Anglican Orders. By Canon Williams. 12mo., 3s. 6d.

R. Washbourne, 18 Paternoster Row, London.

Anglicanism, Harmony of. *See* Marshall (T. W. M.).
Are You Safe in the Church of England? A Question for Anxious Ritualists. By an Ex-Member of the Congregation of S. Bartholomew, Brighton. 8vo., 6d.
ARNOLD (Miss M. J.), Personal Recollections of Cardinal Wiseman, with other Memories. 12mo., 2s. 6d.
ARRAS (Madame d') The Two Friends; or Marie's Self-Denial. 12mo., 1s.; gilt edges, 1s. 6d.
Ars Rhetorica. Auctore R. P. Martino du Cygne. 12mo., 3s.
Artist of Collingwood. 12mo.. 2s.
Association of Prayers. *See* Tondini (Rev. C.).
Augustine (St.) of Canterbury, Life of. 12mo., 3s. 6d.
Aunt Margaret's Little Neighbours; or, Chats about the Rosary. 12mo., 3s.
BAGSHAWE (Rev. J. B.), Catechism of Christian Doctrine, illustrated with passages from the Holy Scriptures. 2s. 6d.
——— Threshold of the Catholic Church. A Course of Plain Instructions for those entering her Communion. 12mo., 4s.
BAGSHAWE (Rt. Rev. Dr.), The Life of our Lord, commemorated in the Mass. 18mo., 6d., bound 1s.; Verses and Hymns separately. 1d., bound 4d.
BAKER (Fr., O.S.B.), The Rule of S. Benedict. From the old English edition of 1638. 12mo., 4s. 6d.
Baker's Boy; or, Life of General Drouot. 18mo., 6d.
BAMPFIELD (Rev. G.), Sir Ælfric and other Tales. 18mo., 6d.; cloth. 1s.; gilt, 1s. 6d.
BARGE (Rev. T.), Occasional Prayers for Festivals. 32mo.. 4d. and 6d.; gilt, 1s.
Battista Varani (B.), *see* Veronica (S.). 12mo., 5s.
Battle of Connemara. By Kathleen O'Meara. 12mo., 3s.
BAUGHAN (Rosa), Shakespeare. Expurgated edition. 8vo., 6s. The Comedies only, 3s. 6d.
Before the Altar. 32mo., 6d.
BELL'S Modern Reader and Speaker. 12mo.. 3s. 6d.
BELLECIO (Fr.), Spiritual Exercises of S. Ignatius. Translated by Dr. Hutch. 18mo., 2s.
BELLINGHAM (Lady Constance) The Duties of Christian Parents. Conferences by Père Matignon. Translated. 12mo., 5s.
Bells of the Sanctuary,—A Daughter of St. Dominick. By Grace Ramsay. 12mo.. 1s. and 1s. 6d.; stronger bound, 2s.
Benedict (S.), Abridged Explanation of his Medal. 1d.
——— The Rule of our most Holy Father S. Benedict, Patriarch of Monks. From the old English edition of 1638. Edited in Latin and English by one of the Benedictine Fathers of St. Michael's, near Hereford. 12mo., 4s. 6d.
Benedictine Breviary. 4 vols., 18mo., Dessain, 1870. 26s. nett; morocco, 42s. nett, and 47s. nett.
Benedictine Missal. Pustet, Folio, 1873. 20s. nett; morocco, 50s. nett, and 60s. nett. Dessain, 4to., 1862, 18s. nett; morocco, 40s. nett, and 50s. nett.

R. Washbourne, 18 Paternoster Row, London.

BENNI (Most Rev. C. B.), Tradition of the Syriac Church of Antioch, concerning the Primacy and Prerogatives of S. Peter and of his successors, the Roman Pontiffs. 8vo., 7s. 6d.

BENVENUTO BAMBOZZI (Fr., O.M.C.), of the Conventual Friars Minor, Life of, from the Italian (2nd edition) of Fr. Nicholas Treggiari, D.D. 12mo., 5s. *In the Press.*

Berchmans (Bl. John), New Miracle at Rome, through the intercession of Bl. John Berchmans. 12mo., 2d.

Bernardine (St.) of Siena, Life of. With Portrait. 12mo., 5s.

Bertha ; or, the Consequences of a Fault. 8vo., 2s. 6d.

Bessy ; or, the Fatal Consequence of Telling Lies. 12mo., 1s.; stronger bound, 1s. 6d.; gilt, 2s.

BESTE (J. R. Digby, Esq.), Catholic Hours. 32mo., 2s ; red edges, 2s. 6d. ; roan, 3s. ; morocco, 6s.

———— Church Hymns. (Latin and English.) 32mo., 6d.

———— Holy Readings. 32mo., 2s , 2s. 6d. ; roan, 3s. ; mor., 6s.

BESTE (Rev. Fr.), Victories of Rome. 8vo., 1s.

Bible. Douay Version. 12mo., 3s. ; Persian, 8s. ; morocco, 10s. 6d. 18mo., 2s. 6d. ; Persian, 5s.; calf or morocco, 7s.; gilt, 8s. 6d. 8vo. with borders round pages, Persian calf, 21s., morocco, 25s. 4to., Illustrated, cloth, 21s.; leather extra, 31s. 6d.; Illustrated, morocco, £5 5s. ; superior, £6 6s.

Bible History for the use of Schools. By Gilmour. 12mo., 2s.

———————— By a Teacher. 12mo., 5s.

Blessed Lord. *See* Ribadeneira ; Rutter (Rev. H.).

Blessed Virgin, Devotions to. From Ancient Sources. *See* Regina Sæculorum. 12mo., 1s. and 3s.

———— Devout Exercise in honour of. From the Psalter and Prayers of S. Bonaventure, 32mo., 1s.

———— History of. By Orsini. Translated by Provost Husenbeth. Illustrated, 12mo., 3s. 6d.

———— Life of. In verse. By C. E. Tame, Esq. 16mo., 2s.

———— Life of. Proposed as a model to Christian women. 12mo., 1s.

———— in North America, Devotion to. By Fr. Macleod. 5s.

———— Veneration of. By Mrs. Stuart Laidlaw. 16mo., 4d.

———— *See* Our Lady, p. 22 ; Leaflets, p. 16 ; May, p. 19.

Blindness, Cure of, through the Intercession of Our Lady and S. Ignatius. 12mo., 2d.

BLOSIUS, Spiritual Works of :—The Rule of the Spiritual Life ; The Spiritual Mirror ; String of Spiritual Jewels. Edited by Rev. Fr. Bowden. 12mo., 3s. 6d. ; red edges, 4s.

Blue Scapular, Origin of. 18mo., 1d.

BLYTH (Rev. Fr.), Devout Paraphrase on the Seven Penitential Psalms. To which is added "Necessity of Purifying the Soul," by St. Francis de Sales. 18mo., 1s. stronger bound, 1s. 6d.; red edges, 2s.

BONA (Cardinal), Easy Way to God. Translated by Father Collins. 12mo., 3s.

BONAVENTURE (S.), Devout Exercise in honour of Our Lady. 32mo., 1s.

BONAVENTURE (S.), Life of St. Francis of Assisi. 3s. 6d.
Boniface (S.), Life of. By Mrs. Hope. 12mo., 6s.
BORROMEO (S. Charles), Rules for a Christian Life. 2d.
BOUDON (Mgr.), Book of Perpetual Adoration. Translated by Rev. Dr. Redman. 12mo., 3s.; red edges, 3s. 6d.
BOUDREAUX (Rev. J., S.J.), God our Father. 12mo., 4s.
——— Happiness of Heaven. 12mo., 4s.
——— Paradise of God. 12mo., 4s.
BOURKE (Rev. Ulick J.), Easy Lessons : or, Self-Instruction in Irish. 12mo., 2s. 6d.
BOWDEN (Rev. Fr. John), Spiritual Works of Louis of Blois. 12mo., 3s. 6d.; red edges, 4s.
——— Oratorian Lives of the Saints. (Page 22).
BOWDEN (Mrs.), Lives of the First Religious of the Visitation of Holy Mary. 2 vols., 12mo., 10s.
BOWLES (Emily), Eagle and Dove. Translated from the French of Mdlle. Zénaïde Fleuriot. 12mo., 2s. 6d. and 5s.
BRADBURY (Rev. Fr.), Journey of Sophia and Eulalis to the Palace of True Happiness. 12mo., 1s. 6d.; 3s. 6d
BRICKLEY'S Standard Table Book. 32mo., ½d.
BRIDGES (Miss), Sir Thomas Maxwell and his Ward. 12mo., 1s. and 2s.
Bridget (S.), Life of, and other Saints of Ireland. 12mo., 1s.
Brigit (S.) Life of, &c. By M. F. Cusack. 8vo., 6s.
Broken Chain. A Tale. 18mo., 6d.
BROWNE (E. G. K., Esq.), Monastic Legends. 8vo., 6d.
BROWNLOW (Rev. W. R. B.), Church of England and its Defenders. 8vo., 1st letter, 6d.; 2nd letter, 1s.
——— "Vitis Mystica"; or, the True Vine : a Treatise on the Passion of our Lord. 18mo., 4s.; red edges, 4s. 6d.
BUCKLEY (Rev. M.), Sermons, Lectures, &c. 12mo., 6s.
BURDER (Abbot), Confidence in the Mercy of God. By Mgr. Languet. 12mo., 3s.
——— The Consoler; or, Pious Readings addressed to the Sick and all who are afflicted. By Père Lambilotte. 12mo., 4s. 6d.; red ed., 5s.
——— Souls in Purgatory. 32mo., 3d.
——— Novena for the Souls in Purgatory. 32mo., 3d.
Burial of the Dead. For Children and Adults. (Latin and English.) Clear type edition, 32mo., 6d.; roan, 1s. 6d.
Burke (Edmund), Life of. *See* Robertson (Professor).
BURKE (S.H., M.A.), Men and Women of the English Reformation. 12mo., 2 vols., 13s.; Vol. II., 5s.
BURKE (Rev. T. N.), Lectures and Sermons. 2 vols., 24s.
BURKE (Father), and others, Catholic Sermons. 12mo.,2s.
BUTLER (Alban), Lives of the Saints. 2 vols., 8vo., 28s.; gilt, 34s.; 4 vols., 8vo., 32s.; gilt, 50s.; leather, 64s.
——— One Hundred Pious Reflections. 18mo., 1s. and 2s.
BUTLER (Dr.), Catechisms. 1st, ½d.; 2nd, 1d.; 3rd, 1½d.
CALIXTE—Life of the Ven. Anna Maria Taigi. Translated by A. V. Smith Sligo. 8vo., 2s. 6d. and 5s.

R. Washbourne, 18 *Paternoster Row, London.*

Callista. Dramatised by Dr. Husenbeth. 12mo., 2s.
Captain Rougemont ; or, the Miraculous Conversion. 8vo., 2s. 6d.
Cassilda ; or, the Moorish Princess of Toledo. 8vo., 2s. 6d.
Catechisms—The Catechism of Christian Doctrine. Good large type on superfine paper. 32mo., 1d., cloth, 2d.; interleaved, 8d.
—— The Catechism of Christian Doctrine. Illustrated with passages from the Holy Scriptures. By the Rev. J. B. Bagshawe. 12mo., 2s. 6d.
—— made Easy. ByRev. H. Gibson. Vol. II, 4s.; Vol. III., 4s.
—— for First Confession. By Rev. R. G. Davis. 32mo., 1d.
—— Lessons on Christian Doctrine. 18mo., 1½d.
—— General Catechism of the Christian Doctrine. By the Right Rev. Bishop Poirier. 18mo., 9d.
—— By Dr. Butler. 32mo., 1st, ½d.; 18mo., 2nd, 1d.; 3rd, 1½d.
—— By Dr. Doyle. 18mo., 1½d.
—— Fleury's Historical. Complete Edition. 18mo., 1½d.
—— Frassinetti's Dogmatic. 12mo., 3s.
—— of the Council. 12mo., 2d.
—— of Perseverance. By Abbé Gaume. 12mo., Vol. I., 7s. 6d.
Catherine Hamilton. By M. F. S. 12mo., 2s. 6d.; gilt, 3s.
Catherine Grown Older. By M. F. S. 12mo., 2s. 6d.; gilt, 3s.
Catholic Hours. *See* Beste (J. R. Digby).
Catholic Keepsake. A Gift Book for all Seasons. 12mo., 6s.
Catholic Piety. *See* Prayer Books, page 30.
Catholic Sick and Benefit Club. *See* Richardson (Rev. R.).
CHALLONER (Bishop), Grounds of Catholic Doctrine Large type edition. 18mo., 4d.
—— Memoirs of Missionary Priests. 8vo., 6s.
—— Think Well on't. 18mo., 2d.; cloth, 6d.
CHAMBERS (F.), The Fair Maid of Kent. An Historica and Biographical Sketch. 8vo., 6d.
Chances of War. An Irish Tale. By A. Whitelock. 8vo., 5s.
CHARDON (Abbe), Memoirs of a Guardian Angel. 4s.
Chats about the Rosary. *See* Aunt Margaret's Little Neighbours.
CHAUGY (Mother Frances Magdalen de), Lives of the First Religious of the Visitation. 2 vols., 12mo., 10s
Child (The). *See* Dupanloup (Mgr.).
Child's Book of the Passion of Our Lord. 32mo., 6d.
Child (The) of Mary's Manual. Second edition, 32mo. 1s.
Children of Mary in the World, Association of. 32mo., 1d.
Choir, Catholic, Manual. By C. B. Lyons. 12mo., 1s.
Christ bearing His Cross. A Steel Engraving from the Picture miraculously given to Blessed Colomba, with a short account of her Life. 8vo., 6d.; proofs, 1s.
CHRISTIAN BROTHERS' Reading Books.
Christian Doctrine, Lessons on. 18mo., 1½d.
Christian, Duties of a. By Ven. de la Salle. 12mo., 2s
Christian Politeness. By the same Author. 18mo., 1s.
Christian Teacher. By the same Author. 18mo., 1s. 8d.
Christmas Offering. 32mo., 1s. a 100 ; or 7s. 6d. for 1000.
Christmas (The First) for our dear Little Ones. 4to., 5s.

Chronological Sketches. *See* Murray Lane (H.).
Church Defence. *See* Marshall (T. W. M.).
Church History. By Alzog. 8vo., 3 vols. each 20s.
——————— By Darras. 4 vols., 8vo., 48s.
——————— Compendium. By Noethen. 12mo., 8s.
——————— for Schools. By Noethen. 12mo., 5s. 6d.
Church of England and its Defenders. *See* Brownlow (Rev.).
Cistercian Legends of the XIII. Century. *See* Collins (Fr.).
Cistercian Order: its Mission and Spirit. *See* Collins (Fr.).
Civilization and the See of Rome. *See* Montagu (Lord).
Clare (Sister Mary Cherubini) of S. Francis, Life of. Preface by Lady Herbert. With Portrait. 12mo., 3s. 6d.
Cloister Legends; or, Convents and Monasteries in the Olden Time. 12mo., 4s.
COGERY (A.), Third French Course, with Vocabulary. 12mo., 2s.
COLLINS (Rev. Fr.), Cistercian Legends of the XIII. Century. 12mo., 3s. [3s. 6d.
——————— Cistercian Order: its Mission and Spirit. 12mo.,
——————— Easy Way to God. Translated from the Latin of Cardinal Bona. 12mo., 3s.
——————— Spiritual Conferences on the Mysteries of Faith and the Interior Life. 12mo., 5s.
COLOMBIERE (Father Claude de la), The Sufferings of Our Lord. Sermons preached in the Chapel Royal, St. James's, in the year 1677. Preface by Fr. Doyotte, S.J. 18mo., 1s.; stronger bound, 1s. 6d.; red edges, 2s.
Colombini (B. Giovanni), Life of. By Belcari. Translated from the editions of 1541 and 1832. With Portrait. 12mo., 3s. 6d.
Columba (S.) Life of, &c. By M. F. Cusack. 8vo., 6s.
Columbkille, or Columba (S.), Life and Prophecies of. By St. Adamnan. 12mo., 3s. 6d.
Comedy of Convocation in the English Church. Edited by Archdeacon Chasuble. 8vo., 2s. 6d. *See* page 18.
COMERFORD (Rev. P.), Handbook of the Confraternity of the Sacred Heart. 18mo., 3d.
——————— Month of May for all the Faithful; or, a Practical Life of the Blessed Virgin. 32mo., 1s.
——————— Pleadings of the Sacred Heart. 18mo., 1s.; gilt, 2s.; with the Handbook of the Confraternity, 1s. 6d.
Communion, Prayers for, for Children. Preparation, Mass before Communion, Thanksgiving. 32mo. 1d.
Compendious Statement of the Scripture Doctrine regarding the Nature and chief Attributes of the Kingdom of Christ. By C. F. A. 8vo., 1s.
COMPTON (Herbert), Semi-Tropical Trifles. 12mo., boards, 1s.; extra cloth, 2s. 6d.
Conferences. *See* Collins, Lacordaire, Mermillod, Ravignan.
Confession, Auricular. By Rev. Dr. Melia. 18mo., 1s. 6d.
Confession and Holy Communion: Young Catholic's Guide. By Dr. Kenny. 32mo., 4d.; cloth, 6d.; red edges, 9d.; French morocco, 1s. 6d.; calf or morocco, 2s. 6d.

R. Washbourne, 18 *Paternoster Row, London.*

Confidence in God. By Cardinal Manning. 16mo., 1s.
Confidence in the Mercy of God. By Mgr. Languet. Translated by Abbot Burder. 12mo., 3s.
Confirmation, Instructions for the Sacrament of. A very complete book. 18mo., 3d.
CONSCIENCE (Hendrick), The Amulet. 12mo., 4s.
—————— The Conscript and Blind Rosa. 12mo., 4s.
—————— Count Hugo, of Graenhove. 12mo., 4s.
—————— The Fisherman's Daughter. 12mo., 4s.
—————— Happiness of being Rich. 12mo., 4s.
—————— Ludovic and Gertrude. 12mo., 4s.
—————— The Village Innkeeper. 12mo., 4s.
—————— Young Doctor. 12mo., 4s.
Consoler (The). By Abbot Burder. 12mo., 4s. 6d. and 5s.
Contemplations on the most Holy Sacrament of the Altar; or Devout Meditations to serve as Preparations for, and Thanksgiving after, Communion. Drawn chiefly from the Holy Scriptures. 18mo., 1s. and 2s.; red edges, 2s. 6d.
Continental Fish Cook. By M. J. N. de Frederic. 18mo., 1s.
Conversion of the Teutonic Race. By Mrs. Hope. 2 vols. 10s.
Convert Martyr; or, "Callista." By the Rev. Dr. Newman. Dramatised by Rev. Dr. Husenbeth. 12mo., 2s.
Convocation, Comedy of. By the Author of "The Oxford Undergraduate of Twenty Years Ago." 8vo. 2s. 6d.
CORTES (John Donoso), Essays on Catholicism, Liberalism, and Socialism. 12mo., 5s.
CRASSET'S Devout Meditations. Translated. 12mo., 8s.
Crests, The Book of Family. Comprising nearly every bearing and its blazonry, Surnames of Bearers, Dictionary of Mottoes, British and Foreign Orders of Knighthood, Glossary of Terms, and upwards of 4,000 Engravings, Illustrative of Peers, Baronets, and nearly every Family bearing Arms in England, Wales, Scotland, Ireland, and the Colonies, &c. 2 vols., 12mo., 24s.
Crucifixion, The. A large picture for School walls, 1s.
CULPEPPER. Family Herbal, 3s. 6d.; coloured plates, 5s. 6d.
CUSACK (M. F.):—Sister Mary Francis Clare.
  Book of the Blessed Ones. 12mo., 4s. 6d.
  Devotions for Public and Private Use at the Way of the Cross. Illustrated. 32mo., 1s.; red edges, 1s. 6d.
  Father Mathew, Life of. 12mo., 2s. 6d. [2s. 6d.
  Good Reading for Sundays and Festivals. 12mo.,
  Ireland, Patriot's History of. 18mo., 2s.
  Jesus and Jerusalem; or, the Way Home. 12mo., 4s. 6d.
  Joseph (S.), Life of. 32mo., 1s.
  Life of the Most Rev. Dr. Dixon. 12mo. 7s. 6d.
  Lives of St. Columba and St. Brigit. 8vo., 6s.
  Mary O'Hagan, Abbess, Life of. 8vo., 6s.
  Memorare Mass. 32mo., 2d.
  Ned Rusheen. 12mo., 5s.
  Nun's Advice to her Girls. 12mo., 2s. 6d.
  O'Connell; his Life and Times. 2 vols. 8vo., 18s

Patrick (S.), Life of. 8vo., 6s., gilt, 10s. ; 32mo., 1s. Illustrated by Doyle (large edition), 4to., 20s.
Patrick's (S.) Manual. 18mo., 3s. 6d.
Pilgrim's Way to Heaven. 12mo., 4s. 6d.
Stations of the Cross, for Public and Private Use. Illustrated. 16mo., 1s.; red edges, 1s. 6d.
The Liberator ; his Public Speeches and Letters. 2 vols. 8vo., 18s.
The Spouse of Christ. 12mo., vol. 2, 7s. 6d.
Tim O'Halloran's Choice. 12mo., 3s. 6d.
Tronson's Conferences. 12mo., 4s. 6d.
DARRAS (Abbe), History of the Church. 4 vols., 8vo., 48s.
Daughter (A) of S. Dominick: (Bells of the Sanctuary). By Grace Ramsay. 12mo., 1s. and 1s. 6d. ; better bound, 2s.
DAVIS (F.), Earlier and Later Leaves ; or, an Autumn Gathering. Poems and Songs. 12mo., 6s.
DAVIS (Rev. R. G.) Catechism for First Confession.' 1d.
—————— Garden of the Soul. *See* page 32.
DEAN (Rev. J. Joy), Devotion to Sacred Heart. 12mo., 2s.
DECHAMPS (Mgr.), The Life of Pleasure. 12mo., 1s. 6d.
DE DOSS (P. A., S.J.), The Pearl among the Virtues ; 3s.
Defence of the Roman Church. *See* Gueranger.
DEHAM (Rev. F.) Sacred Heart of Jesus, offered to the Piety of the Young engaged in Study. 32mo., 6d.
Diary of a Confessor of the Faith. 12mo., 1s.
Directorium Asceticum. By Scaramelli. 4 vols., 12mo., 24s.
DIXON (Fr., O.P.) Albert the Great: his Life and Scholastic Labours. From original documents. By Dr. Sighart. With Photographic Portrait. 8vo. 10s. 6d. Cheap edition, 5s.
—————— Life of St. Vincent Ferrer. From the French of Rev. Fr. Pradel. With a Photograph. 12mo., 5s.
DOYLE (Canon, O.S.B.), Life of Gregory Lopez, the Hermit. With a Photographic Portrait. 12mo., 3s. 6d.
DOYLE (Dr.), Catechism. 18mo., 1½d.
DOYOTTE (Rev. Fr., S.J.), Elevations to the Heart of Jesus. 12mo., 3s.
—————— Sufferings of Our Lord. *See* Columbiere (Fr.)
DRAMAS, &c.—Convert Martyr; or, "Callista" dramatised. 2s.
—————— The Duchess Transformed. By W. H. A. (Girls, 1 Act). A Comedy. 12mo., 6d.
—————— Ernscliff Hall (Girls, 3 Acts). Drama. 12mo., 6d.
—————— Filiola (Girls, 4 Acts). Drama. 12mo., 6d.
—————— He would be a Lord (Boys, 3 Acts), a Comedy. 2s.
—————— Major John Andre [Historical] (Boys, 5 Acts), 2s.
—————— Reverse of the Medal (Girls, 4 Acts). Drama. 6d.
—————— Shandy Maguire (Boys, 2 Acts), a Farce. 12mo., 2s.
—————— St. Eustace (Boys, 5 Acts). Drama. 12mo., 1s.
—————— St. Louis in Chains (Boys, 5 Acts). Drama. 12mo., 2s.
—————— St. William of York (Boys, 2 Acts). Drama. 12mo., 6d.
—————— Whittington and his Cat. Drama for Children. 9 Scenes. By Henrietta Fairfield. 6d.
—————— *See* Shakespeare.

R. *Washbourne*, 18 *Paternoster Row, London.*

Duchess (The), Transformed. By W. H. A. 12mo., 6d.
DUMESNIL (Abbe), Recollections of the Reign of Terror. 12mo., 2s. 6d.
DUPANLOUP (Mgr.), Contemporary Prophecies. 8vo., 1s.
——— The Child. Translated by Kate Anderson. 12mo., 3s. 6d.
Dusseldorf Gallery. 357 Engravings. Large 4to. Half-morocco, gilt, £5 5s. nett.
——— 134 Engravings. Large 8vo. Half-morocco, gilt, 42s.
Dusseldorf Society for the Distribution of Good Religious Pictures. Subscription, 8s. 6d. a year. *Catalogue* 3d.
Duties of a Christian. By Ven. de la Salle. 12mo., 2s.
Eagle and Dove. *See* Bowles (Emily).
E. A. M. Countess Adelstan. 12mo., 1s. and 2s. 6d.
——— Paul Seigneret. 12mo., 6d., 1s., 1s. 6d., gilt, 2s.
——— Regina Sæculorum. 12mo., 1s. and 3s.
——— Rosalie. 12mo., 1s., 1s. 6d., gilt, 2s.
Easy Way to God. By Cardinal Bona. 12mo., 3s.
Ebba ; or, the Supernatural Power of the Blessed Sacrament. *This book is in French.* 12mo., 1s. 6d. ; cloth, 2s. 6d.
Electricity and Magnetism ; an Enquiry into the Nature and Results of. By Amyclanus. Illustrated. 12mo., 6s. 6d.
England, History of. *See* Evans.
Epistles and Gospels. Good clear type edition, 32mo., 6d.; roan, 1s. 6d.; larger edition, 18mo., French morocco, 2s.
———, Explanation of. By Rev. F. Goffine. Illustrated, 8vo., 9s.
Epistles of S. Paul, Exposition of. *See* MacEvilly (Rt. Rev. Dr.)
Ernscliff Hall. A Drama in Three Acts, for Girls. 12mo., 6d.
Eucharistic Year. 18mo., 4s.
Eucharist (The) and the Christian Life. *See* La Bouillerie.
Europe, Modern, History of. With Preface by Bishop Weathers. 12mo., 5s.; roan, 5s. 6d.; cloth gilt, 6s.
Eustace (St.). A Drama in 5 Acts for Boys. By Rev. T. Meyrick, M.A. 12mo., 1s.
EVANS (L.), History of England, adapted for Junior Classes in Schools. 9d., or separately : Part 1 (Standard 4) 2d. Part 2 (Standard 4) 2d. Part 3 (Standard 5) 3d.
——— Chronological Outline of English History. 1½d.
——— Milton's l'Allegro (Oxford Local Exam.). 2d.
——— Parsing and Analysis Table. 1d.
FAIRFIELD (Henrietta), Whittington and his Cat. A Drama, in 9 Scenes, for Children. 12mo., 6d.
Fairy Ching (The); or, the Chinese Fairies' Visit to England. By Henrica Frederic. 12mo., 1s. ; gilt edges, 1s. 6d.
Fairy Tales for Little Children. By Madeleine Howley Meehan. 12mo., 6d.; stronger bound, 1s. and 1s. 6d.; gilt, 2s.
Faith of Our Fathers. *See* Gibbons (Most Rev. Archbishop).
Fall, Redemption, and Exaltation of Man. 12mo., 1s.
Familiar Instructions on Christian Truths. By a Priest. 12mo., 10d.
FARRELL(Rev.J.), Lectures of a certain Professor. 7s. 6d.
FAVRE (Abbe), Heaven Opened by the Practice of Frequent Confession and Communion. 12mo., 2s. ; stronger bound, 3s. 6d.; red edges, 4s.

R Washbourne, 18 Paternoster Row, London.

Feasts (The) of Camelot, with the Tales that were told there. By Mrs. T. K. Hervey. 12mo., 3s. 6d., or in 2 vols. 1s. each.

FERRIS (Rev. D.), Life of St. Mary Frances of the Five Wounds of Jesus Christ. From the Italian. 12mo., 3s. 6d.

Filiola. A Drama in Four Acts, for Girls. 12mo., 6d.

First Apostles of Europe. *See* Hope (Mrs.).

First Communion and Confirmation Memorial. Beautifully printed in gold and colours, folio, 1s. each, or 9s. a dozen, nett.

First Religious of the Visitation of Holy Mary, Lives of. With two Photographs. 2 vols., 12mo., 10s.

FLEET (Charles), Tales and Sketches. 8vo., 2s.; stronger bound, 2s. 6d.; gilt, 3s. 6d.

FLEURIOT (Mlle. Zenaide), Eagle and Dove. Translated by Emily Bowles. 12mo., 2s. 6d. and 5s.

FLEURY'S Historical Catechism. Large edition, 12mo., 1½d.

Flowers of Christian Wisdom. *See* Henry (Lucien).

Fluffy. A Tale for Boys. By M. F. S. 12mo., 3s. 6d.

Following of Christ. *See* A'Kempis.

Foreign Books. *See* R. W.'s Catalogue of Foreign Books. 3d.

Francis of Assisi (S.) Life of. By S. Bonaventure. Translated by Miss Lockhart. 12mo., 3s. 6d.

FRANCIS OF SALES (S.), Consoling Thoughts. 18mo., 2s.

—————— **The Mystical Flora ; or, the Christian Life under the Emblem of Saints.** 4to., 8s.

—————— **Necessity of Purifying the Soul.** *See* Blyth (Rev. Fr.).

—————— **Sweetness of Holy Living.** 18mo., 1s.; levant, 3s.

Franciscan Annals and Monthly Bulletin of the Third Order of St. Francis. 8vo., 6d.

FRANCO (Rev. S.) Devotions to the Sacred Heart. 12mo., 4s.; cheap edition, 2s.

FRASSINETTI—Dogmatic Catechism. 12mo., 3s.

FREDERIC (Henrica), The Fairy Ching ; or, the Chinese Fairies' Visit to England. 12mo., 1s.; gilt edges, 1s. 6d.

FREDERIC (M. J. N. de), Continental Fish Cook ; or, a Few Hints on Maigre Dinners. 18mo., 1s., soiled covers, 6d.

Freemasons, Irish and English, and their Foreign Brothers. 4to., 2s.

From Sunrise to Sunset. By L. B. 12mo., 3s. 6d.

GALLERY (Rev. D.), Handbook of Essentials in History and Literature, Ancient and Modern. 18mo., 1s.

Garden of the Soul. *See* page 32.

Garden (Little) of the Soul. *See* page 30.

Gathered Gems from Spanish Authors. *See* Monteiro.

GAUME (Abbe), Catechism of Perseverance. 4 vols., 12mo. Vol. 1, 7s. 6d.

GAYRARD (Mme. Paul) Harmony of the Passion. Compiled from the four Gospels, in Latin and French. 18mo., 1s. 6d.

German (S.), Life of. 12mo., 3s. 6d.

GIBBONS (Most Rev. Archbishop), The Faith of Our Fathers; Being a Plain Exposition and Vindication of the Church Founded by our Lord Jesus Christ. 12mo., 4s. Paper covers, 2s.

R. Washbourne, 18 *Paternoster Row, London.*

GIBSON (Rev. H.), Catechism made Easy. 12mo., Vol. I. (out of print); Vol. II., 4s. ; Vol. III., 4s.
GILMOUR (Rev. R.), Bible History for the Use of Schools. Illustrated. 12mo., 2s.
God our Father. By a Father of the Society of Jesus. 12mo., 4s.
GOFFINE (Rev. F.), Explanation of the Epistles and Gospels. Illustrated. 8vo., 9s.
Good Thoughts for Priests and People. *See* Noethen.
Gospels, An Exposition of. *See* MacEvilly (Most Rev. Dr.).
Grace before and after Meals. 32mo., 1d. ; cloth, 2d.
GRACE RAMSAY. A Daughter of S. Dominick (Bells of the Sanctuary, No. 4). 12mo., 1s.; stronger bound, 1s. 6d. and 2s.
–––– *See* O'Meara (Kathleen).
GRACIAN (Fr. Baltasar), Sanctuary Meditations for Priests and Frequent Communicants. Translated from the Spanish by Mariana Monteiro. 12mo., 4s.
Grains of Gold. Counsels for the Sanctification and Happiness of Life. 18mo., 1st Series, 6d.; cloth, 1s. 16mo., Series 1 and 2, cloth, 2s. 6d.
GRANT (Bishop), Pastoral on St. Joseph. 32mo., 4d. & 6d.
Gregorian, or Plain Chant and Modern Music. 8vo., 2s. 6d.
Gregory Lopez, the Hermit, Life of. By Canon Doyle, O.S.B. With a Photographic Portrait. 12mo., 3s. 6d.
Grounds of the Catholic Doctrine. By Bishop Challoner. Large type edition, 18mo., 4d.
Guardian Angel, Memoirs of a. By Abbé Chardon. 12mo., 4s.
GUERANGER (Dom), Defence of the Roman Church against F. Gratry. Translated by Canon Woods. 8vo., 1s.
Guide to Sacred Eloquence. *See* Passionist Fathers.
HALL (E.), Munster Firesides. 12mo., 3s. 6d.
Happiness of Being Rich. By Conscience. 12mo., 4s.
Happiness of Heaven. By a Father of the Society of Jesus. 12mo. 4s.
Harmony of Anglicanism. By T. W. Marshall. 8vo., 2s. 6d.
HAY (Bishop), Sincere Christian. 18mo., 2s. 6d.
–––– Devout Christian. 18mo., 2s. 6d.
He would be a Lord. A Comedy in 3 Acts. (Boys). 12mo., 2s.
Heaven Opened by the Practice of frequent Confession and Holy Communion. By the Abbé Favre. 12mo., 2s. ; stronger bound, 3s. 6d.; red edges, 4s.
HEDLEY (Bishop), Five Sermons—Light of the Holy Spirit in the World. 12mo., 1s.; cloth, 1s. 6d. Revelation, Mystery, Dogma and Creeds, Infallibility : separately, 3d. each.
HEIGHAM (John), A Devout Exposition of the Holy Mass. Edited by Austin John Rowley, Priest. 12mo., 4s.
Henri V. (Comte de Chambord). *See* Walsh (W. H.).
HENRY (Lucien), Flowers of Christian Wisdom. 18mo., 1s. and 2s.; red edges, 2s. 6d.
Herbal, Brook's Family. 12mo., 3s. 6d.; coloured plates, 5s. 6d.
HERBERT (Wallace), My Dream and Verses Miscellaneous. With a frontispiece. 12mo., 5s.
–––– The Angels and the Sacraments. 16mo., 1s.

HERGENRÖTHER (Dr.), Anti-Janus. Translated by Professor Robertson. 12mo., 6s.

HERVEY (Eleanora Louisa), My Godmother's Stories from many Lands. 12mo., 3s. 6d.
——— Our Legends and Lives. 12mo., 6s.
——— Rest, on the Cross. 12mo., 3s. 6d.
——— The Feasts of Camelot, with the Tales that were told there. 12mo., 3s. 6d. ; or, separately: Christmas 1s. ; Whitsuntide, 1s.

HILL (Rev. Fr.), Elements of Philosophy, comprising Logic and General Principles of Metaphysics. 8vo., 6s.

HOFFMAN (Franz), Industry and Laziness. 12mo., 3s.

Holy Childhood. A book of simple Prayers and Instructions for very little children. 32mo., 6d. or 1s. ; gilt, 1s. 6d.

Holy Church the Centre of Unity. *See* Shaw (T. H.)

Holy Communion. By Hubert Lebon. 12mo., 4s.

Holy Family, Confraternity of. *See* Manning (Card.).

Holy Places : their Sanctity and Authenticity. *See* Philpin.

Holy Readings. *See* Beste (J. R. Digby Esq.).

HOPE (Mrs.), The First Apostles of Europe ; or, "The Conversion of the Teutonic Race." 2 vols., 12mo., 10s.

Horace. Literally translated by Smart. 18mo., 2s.

HUGUET (Pere), The Power of S. Joseph. Meditations and Devotions. Translated by Clara Mulholland. 1s. 6d.

HUMPHREY (Rev. W., S.J.), The Panegyrics of Fr. Segneri, S.J. Translated from the orignal Italian. With a Preface by the Rev. W. Humphrey, S.J. 12mo., 5s.

HUSENBETH (Rev. Dr.), Convert Martyr. 12mo., 2s.
——— History of the Blessed Virgin. Translated from Orsini. Illustrated. 12mo., 3s. 6d. [Illustrated. 12mo., 5s.
——— Life and Sufferings of Our Lord. By Rev. H. Rutter.
——— Life of Mgr. Weedall. 8vo., 1s.
——— Little Office of the Immaculate Conception. In Latin and English. 32mo., 4d. ; cloth, 6d.; roan, 1s. ; calf or morocco, 2s. 6d.
——— Our Blessed Lady of Lourdes. 18mo., 6d.; with the Novena, 1s.; cloth, 1s. 6d. Novena, separately, 4d.; Litany, 1d.
——— Roman Question. 8vo., 6d.

Husenbeth (Provost), Sermon on his Death. By Very Rev. Canon Dalton. 8vo. 6d.

HUTCH (Rev. W., D D.), Nano Nangle, her Life and her Labours. 12mo., 7s. 6d.

Hymn Book. Complete, for Missions. 32mo., 1d.; cloth, 2d.

Hymn Book (The Catholic). Edited by Rev. G. L. Vere. 32mo., 2d.; cloth, 4d.; Appendix (Hymns to Saints), 1d.

Iceland (Three Sketches of Life in). By Carl Andersen. 12mo.

IGNATIUS (S.), Spiritual Exercises. By Fr. Bellecio, S.J. Translated by Dr. Hutch. 18mo., 2s.

Ignatius (S.), Cure of Blindness through the Intercession of Our Lady and S. Ignatius. 12mo., 2d.

Illustrated Manual of Prayers. 32mo., 3d.; cloth, 4d.
Imitation of Christ. *See* A'Kempis.
Immaculate Conception, Definition of. 12mo., 6d.
―――― Little Office of. *See* Husenbeth (Rev. Dr.).
―――― Little Office of, in Latin and English. 32mo., 1d.
Indulgences. *See* Maurel (Rev. F. A.).
Industry and Laziness. By Franz Hoffman. From the German by James King. 12mo., 3s.
Infallibility of the Pope. By the Author of "The Oxford Undergraduate of Twenty Years Ago." 8vo., 1s.
In Suffragiis Sanctorum. Commem. S. Josephi; Commem. S. Georgii. Set of 5 for 4d.
Insula Sanctorum : The Island of Saints. 12mo., 1s.
Insurrection of '98. By Rev. P. F. Kavanagh. 12mo., 2s. 6d.
IOTA. The Adventures of a Protestant in Search of a Religion : being the Story of a late Student of Divinity at Bunyan Baptist College ; a Nonconformist Minister, who seceded to the Catholic Church. 12mo., 3s. 6d. ; cheap edition, 2s.
Ireland (History of). By Miss Cusack. 18mo., 2s. A large edition, illustrated by Doyle, 8vo., 11s.
Ireland (History of). By T. Young. 18mo., 2s. 6d.
Ireland Ninety Years ago. 12mo., 1s.
Ireland, Popular Poetry of. (Songs). 262 pages, 18mo., 6d.
Ireland, Revelations of, in the Past Generation. 12mo., 1s.
Irish Board Reading Books.
Irish First Book. 18mo., 2d. Second Book. 18mo., 4d.
Irish Monthly. 8vo. Vol. 1877, cloth, 8s.
Italian Revolution (The History of). The History of the Barricades. By Keyes O'Clery, M.P. 8vo., 7s. 6d. and 3s. 6d.
JACOB (W. J.), Personal Recollections of Rome. 6d.
JENKINS (Rev. O. L.) Student's Handbook of British and American Literature. 12mo., 8s.
Jesuits (The), and other Essays. *See* Nevin (Willis, Esq.)
Jesus and Jerusalem ; or, the Way Home. *See* Cusack (Miss).
John of God (S.), Life of. With Photographic Portrait. 12mo., 5s.
Joseph (S.), Life of. By Miss Cusack. 32mo., 6d.; cloth, 1s.
―――― Novena of Meditations. 18mo., 1s.
―――― Novena to, with a Pastoral by the late Bishop Grant. 32mo., 4d.; cloth, 6d.
―――― Power of. *See* Huguet.
―――― *See* Leaflets.
Journey of Sophia and Eulalie to the Palace of True Happiness. From the French by Rev. Fr. Bradbury. 12mo., 1s. 6d.; better bound, 3s. 6d.
KAVANAGH (Rev. P. F.), Insurrection of '98. 1s. 6d.
Keighley Hall, and other Tales. By E. King. 18mo., 6d.; cloth, 1s. ; stronger bound, 1s. 6d. ; gilt, 2s.
KEMEN (Charles), The Marpingen Apparitions. 8vo., 1s.
KENNY (Dr.), Young Catholic's Guide to Confession and Holy Communion. 32mo., 4d.; cloth, 6d.; red edges, 9d.; roan, 1s. 6d.; calf or morocco, 2s. 6d.

R. Washbourne, 18 *Paternoster Row, London.*

KENNY (Dr.), New Year's Gift to our Heavenly Father.
32mo., 4d.
KERNEY (M. T.), Compendium of History. 12mo., 5s.
Key of Heaven. *See* Prayers, page 31.
KINANE (Rev. T. H.), Dove of the Tabernacle. 1s. 6d.
────── Angel (The) of the Altar; or, the Love of the Most Adorable and Most Sacred Heart of Jesus. 18mo., 2s. 3d.
────── Mary Immaculate, Mother of God; or Devotions in honour of the B.V.M. 18mo., 2s.
KING (Elizabeth), Keighley Hall, and other Tales. 18mo., 6d.; cloth, 1s.; stronger bound, 1s. 6d.; gilt, 2s.
────── The Silver Teapot. 18mo., 4d.
KING (James). Industry and Laziness. 12mo., 3s.
Kishoge Papers. Tales of Devilry and Drollery. 12mo., 1s. 6d.
LA BOUILLERIE (Mgr. de), The Eucharist and the Christian Life. Translated by L. C. 12mo., 3s. 6d.
LACORDAIRE'S Conferences. 12mo., On Life, 3s. 6d.; God, 6s.; Jesus Christ, 6s.
Lacordaire. The Inner Life of Pere Lacordaire. From the French of Père Chocarne. 12mo., 6s. 6d.
Lady Mildred's Housekeeper, A Few Words from. 2d.
LAIDLAW (Mrs. Stuart), Letters to my God-child. No. 4. On the Veneration of the Blessed Virgin. 16mo., 4d.
LAING (Rev. Dr.), Blessed Virgin's Root traced in the Tribe of Ephraim. 8vo., 10s. 6d.
────── Descriptive Guide to the Mass. 12mo., 1s. and 1s. 6d.
────── Knight of the Faith. 12mo., 4s.
    Absurd Protestant Opinions concerning *Intention*. 4d.
    Catholic, not Roman Catholic. 4d.
    Challenge to the Churches. 1d.
    Favourite Fallacy about Private Judgment and Inquiry. 1d.
    Protestantism against the Natural Moral Law. 1d.
    What is Christianity? 6d.
    Whence does the Monarch get his right to Rule? 2s. 6d.
LAMBILOTTE (Pere), The Consoler. Translated by Abbot Burder. 12mo., 4s. 6d.; red edges, 5s.
LANGUET (Mgr.), Confidence in the Mercy of God. Translated by Abbot Burder. 12mo., 3s.
Last of the Catholic O'Malleys. By M. Taunton. 18mo., 1s. 6d.; stronger bound, 2s.
Leaflets. 1d. each, or 1s. 2d. per 100 post free.
    Act of Reparation to the Sacred Heart.
    Archconfraternity of the Agonising Heart of Jesus and the Compassionate Heart of Mary: Prayers for the Dying.
    Archconfraternity of Our Lady of Angels.
    Ditto, Rules.
    Christmas Offering (or 7s. 6d. a 1000).
    Devotions to S. Joseph.
    Gospel according to St. John, *in Latin*. 1s. 6d. per 100.
    Indulgenced Prayers for Souls in Purgatory.

R. Washbourne, 18 Paternoster Row, London.

Indulgences attached to Medals, Crosses, Statues, &c., by the Blessing of His Holiness and of those privileged to give his Blessing.
Intentions for Indulgences.
Litany of Our Lady of Angels.
Litany of S. Joseph, and Devotions.
Litany of Resignation.
Miraculous Prayer—August Queen of Angels.
Picture of Crucifixion, " I thirst " (or 5s. a 1000).
Prayer for One's Confessor.
Union of our Life with the Passion of our Lord.
Visit to the Blessed Sacrament. 5s. per 100.

Leaflets. 1d. each, or 6s. per 100.
Act of Consecration to the Sacred Heart.
Concise Portrait of the Blessed Virgin.
Explanation of the Medal or Cross of St. Benedict.
Indulgenced Prayers for the Rosary of the Dead.
Indulgenced Prayer before a Crucifix.
Litany of the Seven Dolours.
Prayer to S. Philip Neri.
Prayers before and after Holy Communion.
Revelation made by the mouth of Our Saviour to St. Bridget.

LEBON (Hubert), Holy Communion. 12mo., 4s.
Legends of the Saints. By M. F. S. 16mo., 3s. 6d.
Lenten Thoughts. By Bishop Amherst. 18mo., 2s.; red edges, 2s. 6d.
LEO XIII., The Church and Civilisation. 8vo., 2s.
Letter to George Augustus Simcox. 8vo., 6d.
Letters to My God-child. By Mrs. Stuart Laidlaw. 16mo., 4d.
Life in the Cloister. By Miss Stewart. 12mo., 3s. 6d.
Life of Pleasure. By Mgr. Dechamps. 12mo., 1s. 6d.
Light of the Holy Spirit in the World. Five Sermons, by Bishop Hedley. 12mo., 1s.; cloth, 1s. 6d.
LIGUORI (S.), Fourteen Stations of the Cross. 18mo., 1d.
——— Selva ; or, a Collection of Matter for Sermons. 12mo., 5s.
——— Way of Salvation. 32mo., 1s.
——— Life of. 12mo., 10s.
——— Officium Parvum. Latin and English. With Novena. 12mo., 1s.; cloth, 2s.; red edges, 3s.
Lily of S. Joseph : A little manual of Prayers and Hymns for Mass. 64mo., 2d.; cloth, 3d., 4d., and 6d.; gilt, 8d.; roan, 1s.; French morocco, 1s. 6d.; calf or morocco, 2s.; gilt, 2s. 6d.
Literature, Philosophy of, An Essay contributing to a. By B. A. M. 12mo., 6s.
Literature, Student's Handbook. See Jenkins (Rev. O. L.).
Little Prayer Book. 32mo., 3d.
Lives of the First Religious of the Visitation of Holy Mary. By Mother Frances Magdalen de Chaugy. With 2 Photographs. 2 vols., 12mo., 10s.
Lost Children of Mount St. Bernard. 18mo., 6d.
Louis (St.), in Chains. Drama, Five Acts (Boys). 12mo., 2s.

Lourdes, Our Blessed Lady of. By Rev. Dr. Husenbeth. 18mo., 6d.; with the Novena, 1s.; cloth, 1s. 6d.
———— Novena of, for the use of the Sick. 4d.
———— Litany of. 1d. each.
———— Photograph, Carte de Visite, 1s.; Cabinet, 2s.; 4to., 4s.
Ludovic and Gertrude. By Conscience. 12mo., 4s.
LUCK (Dom Edmund J.), Short Meditations for every Day in the Year. From the Italian. 12mo. Edition for the Regular Clergy, 2 vols., 9s. ; edition for the Secular Clergy and others, 2 vols., 9s.
LYONS (C. B.), Catholic Choir Manual. 12mo., 1s.
———— Catholic Psalmist. 12mo., 4s. [18mo., 2s.
MACDANIEL (M. A.), Month of May for Interior Souls.
———— Novena to S. Joseph. 32mo., 4d.; cloth, 6d.
———— Road to Heaven. A Game. 3s. 6d.
MACEVILLY (Bishop), Exposition of the Epistles of St. Paul and of the Catholic Epistles. 2 vols., large 8vo. 18s.
———— Exposition of the Gospels. Large 8vo., Vol. I., 12s. 6d.
MACLEOD (Rev. X. D.), Devotion to Our Lady in North America. 8vo., 5s.
Major John Andre. An Historical Drama for Boys. Five Acts. 2s.
MANNING (Cardinal), Church, Spirit and the Word. 6d.
———— Confidence in God. 16mo., 1s.
———— Confraternity of the Holy Family. 8vo., 3d.
———— Glory of S. Vincent de Paul. 12mo., 1s.
———— Independence of the Holy See. 12mo., 5s.
———— True Story of the Vatican Council. 12mo., 5s.
MANNOCK (Patrick), Origin and Progress of Religious Orders, and Happiness of a Religious State. Translated from the Latin of Rev. F. Platus. 12mo., 2s. 6d.
Manual of Catholic Devotions. *See* Prayers, page 31.
Manual of Devotions in honour of Our Lady of Sorrows. Compiled by the Clergy at St. Patrick's, Soho. 18mo., 1s. & 1s. 6d.
Manual of the Cross and Passion. *See* Passionist Fathers.
Manual of the Sisters of Charity. 18mo., 6s.
Margarethe Verflassen. Translated from the German by Mrs. Smith Sligo. 12mo., 1s. 6d. and 3s.; gilt, 3s. 6d.
Margaret Roper. By A. M. Stewart. 12mo., 6s.; extra, 7s.
Marpingen Apparitions. By C. Kemen. 8vo., 1s.
MARQUIGNY (Pere), Life and Letters of Countess Adelstan. 12mo., 1s. and 2s. 6d.
MARSHALL (A. J. P., Esq.), Comedy of Convocation in the English Church. 8vo., 2s. 6d. *
———— English Religion. 8vo. 6d.,
———— Infallibility of the Pope. 8vo., 1s. *
———— Oxford Undergraduate of Twenty Years Ago. 8vo., 2s. 6d.; cloth, 3s. 6d. *
———— Reply to the Bishop of Ripon's Attack on the Catholic Church. 8vo., 6d. *
MARSHALL (T. W. M., Esq.), Harmony of Anglicanism—Church Defence. 8vo., 2s. 6d. *
The 5 (*) in one Volume, 8vo., 6s.

R. Washbourne, 18 *Paternoster Row, London.*

MARSHALL (Rev. W.), The Doctrine of Purgatory. 1s.
MARTIN (Rev. E. R.), Rule of the Pope-King. 8vo., 6d.
Mary, A Remembrance of. 32mo., 2s.
Mary Christina of Savoy (Venerable). 18mo., 6d.
Mary Immaculate, Devotion to. By Rev. T. H. Kinane. 2s.
Mass, Descriptive Guide to. By Rev. Dr. Laing. 12mo., 1s., or stronger bound, 1s. 6d.
Mass, Devotions for. Very *Large type*, 18mo., 2d.
Mass (The). *See* Müller (Rev. M.), Tronson (Abbe).
Mass, A Devout Exposition of. *See* Rowley (Rev. A. J.).
Mathew (Father), Life of. By Miss Cusack. 12mo., 2s. 6d.
Matignon (Pere) The Duties of Christian Parents. 12mo. 5s.
MAUREL (Rev. F. A.), Christian Instructed in the Nature and Use of Indulgences. 18mo., 2s.
Maxims of the Kingdom of Heaven. 12mo., 5s.; red edges, 5s. 6d.: calf or mor., 10s. 6d. Old Testament, 1s. 6d.; Gospels, 1s.
May, Month of. By Rev. P. Comerford. 32mo., 1s.
May, Month of. By M. A. Macdaniel. 18mo., 2s.
May, Month of, principally for the use of Religious Communities. 18mo., 1s. 6d.
May Readings for the Feasts of Our Lady. By Rev. A. P. Bethell. 18mo., 1s. 6d.
M'CORRY (Rev. Dr.), Monks of Iona and the Duke of Argyll. 8vo., 3s. 6d.
—— Rome, Past, Present, Future. 8vo., 6d.
MEEHAN (M. H.), Fairy Tales for Little Children. 12mo., 6d. and 1s.; stronger bound, 1s. 6d.; gilt, 2s.
MELIA (Rev. Dr.), Auricular Confession. 18mo., 1s. 6d.
MERMILLOD (Mgr.), The Supernatural Life. Translated from the French, with a Preface by Lady Herbert. 12mo., 5s.
MEYRICK (Rev. T.), Life of St. Wenefred. 12mo., 2s.
—— St. Eustace. A Drama (5 Acts) for Boys. 12mo., 1s.
M. F. S., Catherine Hamilton. 12mo., 2s. 6d.; gilt, 3s.
—— Catherine Grown Older. 12mo., 2s. 6d.; gilt, 3s.
—— Fluffy. A Tale for Boys. 12mo., 3s. 6d.
—— Legends of the Saints. 16mo., 3s. 6d. [gilt, 1s. 6d.
—— My Golden Days. 12mo., 2s. 6d.; or in 3 vols., 1s. ea.
—— Stories of Holy Lives. 12mo., 3s. 6d.
—— Stories of Martyr Priests. 12mo., 3s. 6d.
—— Stories of the Saints. 12mo., 3s. 6d.; gilt, 4s. 6d.
—————— Second Series. 12mo., 3s. 6d.; gilt, 4s. 6d.
—————— Third Series. 12mo., 3s. 6d.
—— Story of the Life of S. Paul. 12mo., 2s. 6d.
—— The Three Wishes. A Tale. 12mo., 2s. 6d.
—— Tom's Crucifix, and other Tales. 12mo., 3s., or in 5 vols., 1s. each, gilt 1s. 6d.
Message from the Mother Heart of Mary. 18mo., 4d. and 6d.
MILES (G. H.), Truce of God. A Tale. 12mo., 4s.
MILNER (Bishop), Devotion to the Sacred Heart of Jesus. 32mo., 3d.; cloth, 6d.; gilt, 1s.

R. Washbourne, 18 Paternoster Row, London.

Miracles. A New Miracle at Rome, through the intercession of B. John Berchmans. 12mo., 2d.
——— Cure of Blindness, through the intercession of Our Lady and S. Ignatius. 12mo., 2d.
Mirror of Faith—your Likeness in It. By Fr. Hooker. 3s.
Misgivings—Convictions. 12mo., 6d.
Missal. *See* Prayers, page 31.
Monastic Legends. By E. G. K. Browne. 8vo., 6d.
MOHR (Rev. J., S.J.), Cantiones Sacrae. Hymns and Chants. Music and Words. 8vo., 5s.
——— Manual of Sacred Chant. Music and Words. 18mo. 2s. 6d.
MONK (Rev. Fr., O.S.B.), Daily Exercises. 18mo., 3s. 6d.
Monk of the Monastery of Yuste. *See* Monteiro (Mariana).
Monks of Iona and the Duke of Argyll. *See* M'Corry.
MONSABRE (Rev. Pere), Gold and Alloy. 12mo., 2s. 6d.
MONTAGU (Lord Robert), Civilization and the See of Rome. 8vo., 6d.
Montalembert (Count de). By George White. 12mo., 6d.
MONTEIRO (Mariana), Allah Akbar—God is Great. An Arab Legend of the Siege and Conquest of Granada. 12mo., 3s. 6d.
——— Monk of the Monastery of Yuste; or, The Last Days of the Emperor Charles V. An Historical Legend of the 16th Century. 12mo., 2s. 6d.
——— Gathered Gems from Spanish Authors. 12mo., 3s.
——— Sanctuary Meditations. *See* Gracian.
MORA (Ven. Elizabeth Canori), Life of. Translated from the Italian, with Preface by Lady Herbert. With Photograph, 12mo. 3s. 6d.
MULHOLLAND (Rosa), Prince and Saviour: The Story of Jesus. 12mo., Coloured Illustrations, 2s. 6d.; 32mo., 6d.
MULLER (Rev. M.), The Holy Mass. 12mo., 10s. 6d.
Multiplication Table, on a sheet. 3s. per 100.
MURRAY-LANE (Chevalier H.), Chronological Sketch of the Kings of England and the Kings of France. 12mo. 2s. 6d.; or in 2 vols., 1s. 6d. each.
MUSIC: Ave Maria, for Four Voices. By W. Schulthes. 1s. 3d.
 Cæcilian Society. *See* Separate List. Price 1s. or 2s.
 Catholic Hymnal (English Words). For one, two, or four voices, with accompaniment. By Leopold de Prins. 4to., 2s.; bound, 3s.
 Cor Jesu, Salus in Te sperantium. By W. Schulthes, 2s.; with Harp Accompaniment, 2s. 6d.; abridged, 3d.
 Corona Lauretana. 20 Litanies by W. Schulthes. 2s.
 Evening Hymn at the Oratory. By Rev. J. Nary. 3d.
 Litanies (36) and Benediction Service. By W. Schulthes. 6s. Second Series (Corona Lauretana). 2s.
 Litanies (6). By E. Leslie. 6d.
 Litanies (18). By Rev. J. McCarthy. 1s. 3d.
 Litany of the B.V.M. By Baronnesse Emma Freemantle. 6d.
 Mass of the Holy Child Jesus. In Unison. By

W. Schulthes. 3s. The vocal part only, 4d. ; or 3s. per doz. Cloth, 6d.; or 4s. 6d. per doz. [Schaller. 2s. 6d.
Mass of St. Patrick. For three equal voices. By F.
Ne projicias me a facie Tua. Motett for Four Voices. By W. Schulthes. 1s. 3d.
Oratory Hymns. By W. Schulthes. 2 vols., 8s.
Recordare. Oratorio Jeremiæ Prophetæ. By the same. 1s.
Regina Cœli. Motett for Four Voices. By W. Schulthes. 3s. Vocal Arrangement, 1s.
Six Sacred Vocal Pieces, for three or four equal Voices. By W. Schulthes. 4s.
Six Invocations, for four equal Voices. By W. Schulthes. 1s. 6d.
Twelve Latin Hymns. By W. Schulthes. 1s. 6d.
Veni Domine. Motett for Four Voices. By W. Schulthes. 2s. Vocal Arrangement, 6d.
Vespers and Benediction Service. Composed and harmonized by Leopold de Prins. 4to., 3s. 6d.

⁎ *All the above (music) prices are nett.*

My Conversion and Vocation. By Rev. Father Schouvaloff, 5s.
My Godmother's Stories from many Lands. By Mrs. T. K. Hervey. 12mo., 3s. 6d.
My Golden Days. By M. F. S. 12mo., 2s. 6d., or in 3 vols., 1s. each ; or 1s. 6d. gilt.
NARY (Rev. J.) Evening Hymn at the Oratory. Music, 3d.
Necessity of Enquiry as to Religion. *See* Pye (Henry John).
NEVIN (Willis, Esq.), The Jesuits, and other Essays. 12mo., 1s.; cloth, 2s. 6d.
NEWMAN (Rev. Dr.), Miscellanies, 6s.; Critical and Historical Essays, 2 vols., 12s. ; Tracts, Theological and Ecclesiastical, 8s. ; Certain Difficulties felt by Anglicans, second series, 5s. 6d. Via Media, 2 vols., 12s. Development, 6s.
——— **Characteristics from the Writings of.** By W. S. Lilly. 12mo., 6s.
New Testament. 12mo., 2s. 6d. Persian calf, 7s. 6d., morocco, 10s. Illustrated, large 4to., 7s. 6d.
New Year's Gift to Our Heavenly Father. 32mo., 4d.
Nicholas ; or, the Reward of a Good Action. 18mo., 6d.
NICHOLS (T. L.), Forty Years of American Life. 5s.
Nina and Pippo, the Lost Children of Mt. St. Bernard. 6d.
NOETHEN'S (Rev. T.), Good Thoughts for Priests and People ; or, Short Meditations for every Day in the Year. 8s.
——— **Compendium of the History of the Catholic Church.** 12mo., 8s.
——— **History of the Catholic Church.** 12mo., 5s. 6d.
Novena to Our Blessed Lady of Lourdes for the use of the Sick. 18mo., 4d.
Novena of Grace, revealed by S. Francis Xavier. 18mo., 6d.
Novena of Meditations in honour of St. Joseph, according to the method of St. Ignatius, preceded by a new method of hearing Mass according to the intentions of the Souls in Purgatory. 18mo., 1s.

Occasional Prayers for Festivals. *See* Prayers, page 31.
O'CLERY (Keyes, M.P., K.S.G.), The History of the Italian Revolution. First Period—The Revolution of the Barricades (1796-1849). 8vo., 7s. 6d. Cheap edition 3s. 6d.
O'Connell the Liberator. *See* Cusack (M. F.).
O'GALLAGHER (Dr.), Sermons in Irish-Gælic; with literal idiomatic English Translation, and a Memoir of the Bishop, by Canon U. J. Bourke. 8vo., 7s. 6d.
O'Hagan (Mary), Life of. By Miss Cusack. 8vo., 6s.
O'HAIRE (Rev. J.), Recollections of South Africa. 7s. 6d.
O'MAHONY (D.P.M.), Rome semper eadem. 8vo., 1s. 6d.
O'MEARA (Kathleen), The Battle of Connemara. 12mo., 3s.
―――― *See* Grace Ramsay.
On what Authority do I accept Christianity? 12mo., 6d.
Oratorian Lives of the Saints. With Portrait, 12mo., 5s. a vol.
   I. S. Bernardine of Siena, Minor Observatine.
   II. S. Philip Benizi, Fifth General of the Servites.
   III. S. Veronica Giuliani, and B. Battista Varani.
   IV. S. John of God. By Canon Cianfogni.
O'REILLY (Rev. Dr.), Victims of the Mamertine. 5s.
―――――A Romance of Repentance. 12mo., 3s. 6d.
Oremus, A Liturgical Prayer Book. *See* p. 31.
Our Lady's Comfort to the Sorrowful. 32mo., 6d. and 1s.
Our Lady (Devotion to) in North America. *See* Macleod.
Our Lady's Lament. *See* Tame (C.E.).
Our Lady's Month. By Rev. A. P. Bethell. 18mo., 1s. 6d.
Our Legends and Lives. By E. L. Hervey. 12mo., 6s.
Our Lord's Life, Passion, Death, and Resurrection. Translated from Ribadeneira. 12mo., 1s.
―――― By Rev. H. Rutter. Illustrated. 12mo., 5s.
―――― Incidents. A Series of 12 Illuminations. 4to., 6s.
OXENHAM (H. N.), Dr. Pusey's Eirenicon. 8vo., 6d.
―――― Poems. 12mo., 3s. 6d.
Oxford Undergraduate of Twenty Years Ago. By a Bachelor of Arts. 8vo., 2s. 6d.; cloth, 3s. 6d.
OZANAM (A. F.), Protestantism and Liberty. Translated from the French by Wilfrid C. Robinson. 8vo., 1s.
Pale (The) and the Septs. A Romance of the XVI. Century. 6s.
Panegyrics of Fr. Segneri, S.J. Translated from the original Italian. With a Preface, by Rev. W. Humphrey, S.J. 12mo., 5s.
Paradise of God; or the Virtues of the Sacred Heart. By Author of "God our Father," "Happiness of Heaven." 12mo., 4s.
Paray le Monial, and Bl. Margaret Mary. 18mo., 6d.
Passion of Our Lord, Harmony of. *See* Gayrard (Mme.).
PASSIONIST FATHERS: Mirror of Faith. 12mo., 3s.
   Manual of the Cross and Passion. 32mo., 3s.
   Sacred Eloquence. 18mo., 2s.
   S. Paul of the Cross. 12mo., 3s.
   School of Jesus Crucified. 18mo., 5s.
Pastor and People. By Rev. T. J. Potter. 12mo., 5s.
Path to Paradise. *See* Prayers, page 31.
Patrick (S.), Life of. 1s.; 8vo., 6s.; gilt, 10s.; 4to., 20s.

R. Washbourne, 18 *Paternoster Row, London.*

Patrick's (S.) Manual. By Miss Cusack. 18mo., 3s. 6d.
Patron Saints. By E. A. Starr. Illustrated. 12mo., 10s.
Paul of the Cross (S.), Life of. *See* Passionist Fathers.
Pearl among the Virtues. By Rev. P. A. De Doss. 12mo., 3s.
Penitential Psalms. *See* Blyth (Rev. F.).
PENS, Washbourne's Free and Easy. Fine, or Middle, or Broad Points, 1s. per gross.
People's Martyr. A Legend of Canterbury. 12mo., 4s.
Percy Grange. By Rev. T. J. Potter. 12mo., 3s.
Perpetual Adoration, Book of. Boudon. 12mo., 3s. and 3s. 6d.
Peter (S.), his Name and his Office. *See* Allies (T. W., Esq.).
Peter, Years of. By an ex-Papal Zouave. 12mo., 1d.
Philip Benizi (S.), Life of. *See* Oratorian Lives of the Saints.
Philomena (S.), Life and Miracles of. 12mo., 2s. 6d.
Philosophy, Elements of. By Rev. W. H. Hill. 8vo., 6s.
PHILPIN (Rev. F.), Holy Places; their sanctity and authenticity. With three Maps. 12mo., 2s. 6d. and 6s.
Photographs (10) illustrating the History of the Miraculous Hosts, called the Blessed Sacrament of the Miracle. 2s. 6d. the set.
Pius IX. 32mo., 6d.; 4to., 1d.
Pius IX., from his Birth to his Death. By G. White. 12mo., 6d.
Pius IX., his early Life to the Return from Gaeta. By Rev. T. B. Snow, O.S.B. 12mo., 6d.
Plain Chant. *See* Gregorian.
———— The Cecilian Society Music kept in stock.
PLATUS (Rev. F.), Origin and Progress of Religious Orders, and Happiness of a Religious State. 12mo., 2s. 6d.
PLAYS. *See* Dramas, page 10.
POIRIER (Bishop), A General Catechism of the Christian Doctrine. 18mo., 9d.
POOR CLARES OF KENMARE. *See* Cusack (Miss).
Pope-King, Rule of. By Rev. E. R. Martin. 8vo., 6d.
Pope of Rome. *See* Tondini (Rev. C.).
POTTER (Rev. T. J.), Extemporary Preaching. 5s.
———— Farleyes of Farleye. 12mo., 2s. 6d.
———— Pastor and People. 12mo., 5s.
———— Percy Grange. 12mo., 3s.
———— Rupert Aubrey. 12mo., 3s.
———— Sir Humphrey's Trial. 16mo., 2s. 6d.
POWELL (J., Esq.), Two Years in the Pontifical Zouaves. Illustrated. 8vo., 3s. 6d.
PRADEL (Fr., O. P.), Life of St. Vincent Ferrer. Translated by Rev. Fr. Dixon. With a Photograph. 12mo., 5s.
PRAYER BOOKS. *See* page 30.
PRINS (Leopold de). *See* Music.
Pro-Cathedral, Kensington. Tinted View of the Interior, 11 × 15 inches, 1s.; Proofs, on larger paper, 2s.
Prophecies, Contemporary. By Mgr. Dupanloup. 8vo., 1s.
Protestantism and Liberty. *See* Robinson (W. C.).
Protestant Principles examined by the Written Word. 1s.

Prussian Spy. A Novel. By V. Valmont. 12mo., 4s.
Purgatory, A Novena in favour of the Souls in. 32mo., 3d.
Purgatory, Month of the Souls in Purgatory. By Ricard, 1s.
Purgatory, The Doctrine of. By Rev. W. Marshall. 12mo., 1s.
Purgatory, Souls in. By Abbot Burder. 32mo., 3d.
Pusey's (Dr.) Eirenicon considered. *See* Oxenham (H. N.).
PYE (Henry John, M.A.), Necessity of Enquiry as to Religion. 32mo., 4d.; cloth, 6d.
——— The Religion of Common Sense. New Edition. 1s.
——— Are the Ritualists Catholic? 8vo., 6d.
RAMIERE (Rev. H.), Apostleship of Prayer. 12mo., 6s.
RAVIGNAN (Pere), The Spiritual Life, Conferences. Translated by Mrs. Abel Ram. 12mo., 5s.
Ravignan (Pere), Life of. 12mo., 9s.
RAWES (Rev F.), Homeward. 2s. Sursum. 1s.
Reading Lessons. By the Marist Brothers. 12mo., 1st Book, 4d.; 2nd Book, 7d.
REDMAN (Rev. Dr.), Book of Perpetual Adoration. By Mgr. Boudon. 12mo., 3s.; red edges, 3s. 6d. [18mo., 1s.
REDMOND (Rev. Dr.), Eight Short Sermon Essays.
REEVE'S History of the Bible. 12mo., 3s. 6d.
Reflections, One Hundred Pious. *See* Butler.
Regina Sæculorum; or, Mary Venerated in all Ages. Devotions to the Blessed Virgin from Ancient Sources. 12mo., 1s. and 3s.
Rejection of Catholic Doctrines attributable to the Non-Realization of Primary Truths. 8vo., 1s.
Religion of Common Sense. By H. J. Pye, M.A. 12mo., 1s.
Religious Orders. *See* Platus (Rev. F.).
Rest, on the Cross. By Eleanora Louisa Hervey. 12mo., 3s. 6d.
Reverse of the Medal. A Drama for Girls. 12mo., 6d.
RIBADENEIRA—Life, Passion, Death and Resurrection of our Lord. 12mo., 1s.
RICARD (Abbe), Month of the Holy Angels. 18mo., 1s.
——— Month of the Souls in Purgatory. 18mo., 1s.
RICHARDSON (Rev. Fr.), Catholic Sick and Benefit Club; or, the Guild of our Lady; and St. Joseph's Catholic Burial Society. 32mo., 4d.
——— Little by Little; or, the Penny Bank. 32mo., 1d.
——— Shamrocks. 6s. 2d. a gross (144), post free.
——— S. Joseph's Catholic Burial Society. 2d.
——— The Crusade; or, Catholic Association for the Suppression of Drunkenness. 32mo., 1d.
Ritus Servandus in Expositione et Benedictione S.S. 4to., cloth, 5s. 6d.
Road to Heaven. A Game. By Miss M. A. Macdaniel. 3s. 6d.
ROBERTSON (Professor), Lectures on the Life, Writings, and Times of Edmund Burke. 12mo., 3s. 6d.
——— Lectures on Modern History and Biography. 6s.
ROBINSON (Wilfrid C.), Protestantism and Liberty. Translated from the French of Professor Ozanam. 8vo., 1s.
Roman Question, The. By Rev. Dr. Husenbeth. 8vo., 6d.
Rome and her Captors: Letters collected and edited by Count Henri d'Ideville, and Translated by F. R. Wegg-Prosser. 4s.

R. Washbourne, 18 *Paternoster Row, London.*

Rome, Past, Present, and Future. By Dr. M'Corry. 8vo., 6d.
—— Personal Recollections of. By W. J. Jacob, 8vo., 6d.
—— The Victories of. By Rev. F. Beste. 8vo., 1s.
—— (To) and Back. Fly-Leaves from a Flying Tour. Edited by Rev. W. H. Anderdon, S.J., 12mo., 2s.
Rosalie ; or, the Memoir of a French Child, told by herself. 12mo., 1s.; stronger bound, 1s. 6d.; gilt, 2s.
Rosary, Fifteen Mysteries of, and Fourteen Stations of the Cross. In One Volume, 32 Illustrations. 16mo., 2s.
Rosary for the Souls in Purgatory, with Indulgenced Prayer. 6d. and 9d. Medals separately, 1d. each, or 9s. gross. Prayers separately, 1d. each, 9d. a dozen, or 6s. for 100.
Rosary, Chats about the. *See* Aunt Margaret's Little Neighbours.
ROWLEY (Rev. Austin John), A Devout Exposition of the Holy Mass. Composed by John Heigham. 12mo., 4s.
RUSSELL (Rev. M.) Eucharistic Verses. 12mo., 2s.
RUTTER (Rev. H.) Life and Sufferings of Our Lord, with Introduction by Rev. Dr. Husenbeth. Illustrated. 12mo., 5s.
RYAN (Bishop). What Catholics do not Believe. 12mo., 1s.
Sacred Heart, Act of Consecration to. 1d.; or 6s. per 100.
——————, Act of Reparation to. 1s. 2d. per 100.
——————, A Spiritual Banquet. 6d.
——————, Devotions to. By Rev. S. Franco. 12mo., 4s.; cheap edition, 2s. [cloth, 6d.; gilt, 1s.
——————, Devotions to. By Bishop Milner. 32mo., 3d.;
——————, Devotions to. Translated by Rev. J. Joy Dean. 12mo., 2s. [12mo., 3s.
——————, Elevations to the. By Rev. Fr. Doyotte, S.J.
——————, Handbook of the Confraternity, for the use of Members. 18mo., 3d.
——————, Little Treasury of. 32mo., 2s.; French morocco, 2s. 6d.; calf, 5s. ; morocco, 6s.
——————, Manual of Devotions to the, from the writings of Blessed Margaret Mary. 32mo., 3d.
—————— offered to the Piety of the Young engaged in Study. By Rev. F. Deham. 32mo., 6d.
—————— *See* Paradise of God ; Kinane (Rev. T. H.).
—————— Pleadings of. By Rev. M. Comerford. 18mo., 1s.; gilt edges, 2s.; with Handbook of the Confraternity, 1s. 6d.
——————, Treasury of. 18mo., 3s. 6d.; roan, 4s.
Sacred History in Forty Pictures. Plain, 5s.; coloured, 7s. 6d.; mounted on cardboard, coloured, 18s. 6d. and 22s.
Saints, Lives of. By Alban Butler. 4 vols., 8vo., 32s.; gilt, 50s.; and leather, gilt, 64s.; or the 4 vols. in 2, 28s.; gilt, 34s.
—————— for every day in the Year. Beautifully printed, within illustrated borders from ancient sources, on thick toned paper. 4to., gilt, 21s.
—————— Patron. By E. A. Starr. Illustrated. 12mo., 10s.
ST. JURE (S.J.) Knowledge and Love of Jesus Christ. 3 vols., 8vo., 30s.
—————— The Spiritual Man. 12mo., 6s.

R. Washbourne, 18 *Paternoster Row, London.*

Sanctuary Meditations for Priests and Frequent Communicants. Translated from the Spanish of Fr. Baltasar Gracian, by Mariana Monteiro. 12mo., 4s.
SCARAMELLI—Directorium Asceticum; or, Guide to the Spiritual Life. 4 vols. 12mo., 24s. Vols. 4, 3, or 2 sold separately, 6s. each.
SCHMID (Canon), Tales. Illustrated. 12mo., 3s. 6d. Separately:—The Canary Bird, The Dove, The Inundation, The Rose Tree, The Water Jug, The Wooden Cross. 6d. each; gilt, 1s.
SCHOOL BOOKS. Supplied according to order.
School of Jesus Crucified. By the Passionist Fathers. 18mo., 5s.
SCHOUVALOFF (Rev. Father, Barnabite), My Conversion and Vocation. Translated from the French, with an Appendix, by Fr. C. Tondini. 12mo., 5s.
SCHULTHES (William). See Music.
Scraps from my Scrapbook. See Arnold (M. J.).
SEGNERI (Fr., S.J.), Panegyrics. Translated from the original Italian. With a Preface, by Rev. W. Humphrey. 12mo., 5s.
SEGUR (Mgr.), Books for Little Children. Translated. 32mo., 3d. each. Confession, Holy Communion, Child Jesus, Piety, Prayer, Temptation and Sin. In one volume, cloth, 2s.
—— Practical Counsels for Holy Communion. 18mo., 1s.
SEGUR (Countess de), The Little Hunchback. 12mo., 3s.
Seigneret (Paul), Life of. 12mo., 6d., 1s., and 1s. 6d.; gilt, 2s.
Selva; a Collection of Matter for Sermons. By St. Liguori. 12mo., 5s.
Semi-Tropical Trifles. By H. Compton. 12mo., 1s.; cloth, 2s. 6d.
Sermon Essays. By Rev. Dr. Redmond. 12mo., 1s.
Sermons. Irish and English. By Dr. O'Gallagher. 8vo., 7s. 6d.
—— By Father Burke, O.P., and others. 12mo., 2s.
—— The Light of the Holy Spirit in the World. By Bishop Hedley. 1s.; cloth, 1s. 6d.
—— One Hundred Short. By Rev. Fr. Thomas. 8vo., 12s.
Sermons, Lectures, &c. By Rev. M. M. Buckley. 12mo., 6s.
Serving Boy's Manual, and Book of Public Devotions. Containing all those prayers and devotions for Sundays and Holydays, usually divided in their recitation between the Priest and the Congregation. Compiled from approved sources, and adapted to Churches, served either by the Secular or Regular Clergy. 32mo., embossed, 1s.; French morocco, 2s.; calf, 4s.; with Epistles and Gospels, 6d. extra.
Seven Sacraments Explained and Defended. 18mo., 1s. 6d.
SHAKESPEARE. Expurgated edition. By Rosa Baughan. 8vo., 6s. The Comedies only, 3s. 6d.
Shandy Maguire. A Farce for Boys. 2 Acts. 12mo., 2s.
SHAW (T. H.), Holy Church the Centre of Unity; or, Ritualism compared with Catholicism. 8vo., 1s.
Siege of Limerick (Florence O'Neill). See Stewart (Agnes M.).
SIGHART (Dr.) Albertus Magnus. 10s. 6d. Cheap edition, 5s.
Silver Teapot. By Elizabeth King. 18mo., 4d.
Simple Tales—Waiting for Father, &c., &c. 16mo., 2s. 6d.

Sir Ælfric and other Tales. *See* Bampfield (Rev. G.).
Sir Humphrey's Trial. By Rev. T. J. Potter. 16mo., 2s. 6d.
Sir Thomas Maxwell and his Ward. By Miss Bridges. 12mo, 1s. and 2s.
Sisters of Charity, Manual of. 18mo. 6s.
SMITH-SLIGO (A. V., Esq.), Life of the Ven. Anna Maria Taigi. Translated from French of Calixte. 8vo., 2s. 6d. and 5s.
— (Mrs.) Margarethe Verflassen. 12mo., 1s. 6d., 3s., and 3s. 6d.
SNOW (Rev. T. B.), Pius IX., His early Life to the Return from Gaeta. 12mo., 6d.
Soul (The), United to Jesus. 32mo., 1s. 6d.
SPALDING'S (Abp.) Works. 5 vols., 52s. 6d.; or separately Evidences of Catholicity, 10s. 6d.; Miscellanea, 2 vols., 21s.; Protestant Reformation, 2 vols., 21s.; cheap edition, 1 vol., 14s.
Spalding (Archbishop), Life of. 8vo., 10s. 6d.
——— Sermon at the Month's Mind. 8vo., 1s.
Spiritual Conferences on the Mysteries of Faith and the Interior Life. By Father Collins. 12mo., 5s.
Spiritual Life. Conferences by Père Ravignan. Translated by Mrs. Abel Ram. 12mo., 5s.
Spiritual Works of Louis of Blois. Edited by Rev. F. John Bowden. 12mo., 3s. 6d.; red edges, 4s.
Spouse of Christ. By Sister M. F. Clare. 12mo., vol. 2, 7s. 6d.
STARR (Eliza Allen), Patron Saints. Illustrated. 12mo., 10s.
Stations of the Cross, Devotions for Public and Private Use at the. By Miss Cusack. Illustrated. 16mo., 1s. and 1s. 6d.
Stations of the Cross. By S. Liguori. 18mo., 1d.
Stations of the Cross and Mysteries of the Rosary. 2s.
STEWART (A. M.), Alone in the World. 12mo., 4s. 6d.
——— St. Angela's Manual. *See* Angela (S.)
——— Biographical Readings. 12mo., 4s. 6d.
——— Cardinal Wolsey. 12mo., 6s. 6d.
——— Sir Thomas More. Illustrated, 10s. 6d.; gilt, 11s. 6d.
——— Life of S. Angela Merici. 12mo., 4s. 6d.
——— Life in the Cloister. 12mo., 3s. 6d. [extra, 6s.
——— Limerick Veteran; or, the Foster Sisters. 12mo., 5s.;
——— Margaret Roper. 12mo., 6s.; extra, 7s. [16mo., 1s.
Stories for my Children—The Angels and the Sacraments.
Stories of Holy Lives. By M. F. S. 12mo., 3s. 6d.
Stories of Martyr Priests. By M. F. S. 12mo., 3s. 6d.
Stories of the Saints. By M. F. S. 12mo., 1st Series, 3s. 6d.; gilt, 4s. 6d. 2nd Series, 3s. 6d.; gilt, 4s. 6d. 3rd Series, 3s. 6d.
Stormsworth, with other Poems and Plays. By the author of "Thy Gods, O Israel.' 12mo., 3s. 6d.
Story of an Orange Lodge. 12mo., 1s.
Story of Marie and other Tales. 12mo., 2s.; gilt, 3s., or separately:—The Story of Marie, 2d.; Nelly Blane, and a Contrast, 2d.; A Conversion and a Death-bed, 2d.; Herbert Montagu, 2d.; Jane Murphy, the Dying Gipsy, and the Nameless Grave, 2d.; The Beggars, and True and False Riches, 2d.; Pat and his Friend, 2d.

Story of the Life of St. Paul. By M. F. S., author of "Stories of the Saints." 12mo., 2s. 6d.

Sufferings of our Lord. Sermons preached by Father Claude de la Colombière, S.J., in the Chapel Royal, St. James's, in the year 1677. 18mo., 1s.; stronger bound, 1s. 6d.; red edges, 2s.

Supernatural Life, The. By Mgr. Mermillod. Translated from the French, with a Preface by Lady Herbert. 12mo., 5s.

Supremacy of the Roman See. By C. E. Tame, Esq. 8vo., 6d.

Sure Way to Heaven. A Little Manual for Confession and Holy Communion. 32mo., 6d.; Persian, 2s. 6d.; calf or morocco, 3s. 6d.

Sweetness of Holy Living; or, Honey culled from the Flower Garden of S. Francis of Sales. 18mo., 1s.; French morocco, 3s.

Taigi (Anna Maria), Life of. Translated from the French of Calixte by A. V. Smith-Sligo, Esq. 8vo., 2s. 6d. and 5s.

Tales and Sketches. *See* Fleet (Charles).

Tales of the Jewish Church. By Charles Walker. 12mo., 2s. 6d.

TAME (C. E., Esq.), Early English Literature. 16mo., 2s. a vol. I. Our Lady's Lament, and the Lamentation of S. Mary Magdalene. II. Life of Our Lady, in verse.

—————— **Supremacy of the Roman See.** 8vo., 6d.

TANDY (Rev. Dr.), Terry O'Flinn. 12mo., 1s.; stronger bound, 1s. 6d.; gilt, 2s.

TAUNTON (M.), Last of the Catholic O'Malleys. 18mo., 1s. 6d.; stronger bound, 2s.

—————— **One Hundred Pious Reflections,** from Alban Butler's Lives of the Saints. 18mo., 1s.; stronger bound, 2s.

Temperance Books. *See* Richardson (Rev. Fr.).

—————— Cards (Illuminated), 3d. each.   [3d. each.

—————— Medals—Immaculate Conception, St. Patrick, St. Joseph.

Terry O'Flinn. By Rev. Dr. Tandy. 12mo., 1s., 1s. 6d. and 2s.

Testimony; or, the Necessity of Enquiry as to Religion. By John Henry Pye, M.A. 32mo., 4d.; cloth, 6d.

THOMAS (H. J.), One Hundred Short Sermons. 8vo., 12s.

Three Wishes. A Tale. By M. F. S. 12mo., 2s 6d.

Threshold of the Catholic Church. *See* Bagshawe (Rev. J. B.)

Tim O'Halloran's Choice. *See* Cusack.

Tom's Crucifix, and other Tales. By M. F. S. 12mo., 3s., or in 5 vols., 1s. each; gilt, 1s. 6d.

TONDINI (Rev. Cæsarius), My Conversion and Vocation. By Rev. Fr. Schouvaloff. 12mo., 5s.

—————— **The Pope of Rome and the Popes of the Oriental Orthodox Church.** An essay on Monarchy in the Church, with special reference to Russia. Second Edition. 12mo., 3s. 6d.

—————— **Some Documents concerning of the Association Prayers in Honour of Mary Immaculate, for the Return of the Greek-Russian Church to Catholic Unity.** 12mo., 3d. Association of Prayers, 32mo., 1d.

Transubstantiation, Catholic Doctrine of. 12mo., 6d.

Trials of Faith. *See* Browne (E. G. K.).

TRONSON (Abbe), The Mass: a devout Method. 32mo., 4d.

TRONSON'S Conferences for Ecclesiastical Students and
Religious. By Sister M. F. Clare. 12mo., 4s. 6d.
Two Colonels. By Father Thomas. 12mo., 6s. [gilt, 1s. 6d.
Two Friends; or Marie's Self-Denial. By Madame d'Arras. 1s., or
Ursuline Manual. *See* Prayers, page 32.
VALMONT (V.), The Prussian Spy. A Novel. 12mo., 4s.
VAUGHAN (Bishop of Salford), Holy Sacrifice of the
Mass. 2d.; cloth, 6d.
——— Love and Passion of Jesus Christ. 2d.
VERE (Rev. G. L.), The Catholic Hymn Book. 32mo.,
2d.; cloth, 4d. Appendix containing Hymns in honour of Saints. 1d.
Veronica Giuliani (S.), Life of, and B. Battista Varani.
With a Photographic Portrait. 12mo., 5s.
Village Lily. A Tale. 12mo., 1s.; gilt, 1s. 6d.
Vincent Ferrer (S.), of the Order of Friar Preachers; his
Life, Spiritual Teaching, and Practical Devotion.
By Rev. Fr. Andrew Pradel, O.P. Translated from the French by
the Rev. Fr. T. A. Dixon, O.P., with a Photograph. 12mo., 5s.
VINCENT OF LIRINS (S.). Commonitory. 12mo., 1s. 3d.
Vincent of Paul (S.), Glory of. *See* Manning (Archbishop).
VIRGIL. Literally translated by Davidson. 12mo., 2s. 6d.
"Vitis Mystica"; or, the True Vine. *See* Brownlow.
WALKER (Charles), Are You Safe in the Church of
England? 8vo., 6d.
——— Tales of the Jewish Church. 12mo., 2s. 6d.
WALLER (J. F., Esq.), Festival Tales. 12mo., 3s 6d.
Way of Salvation. By S. Liguori. 32mo., 1s.
WEBB(Alfred), Compendium of Irish Biography. 8vo., 16s.
Weedall (Mgr.), Life of. By Rev. Dr. Husenbeth. 8vo., 1s.
WEGG-PROSSER (F. R.), Rome and her Captors. 4s.
Wenefred (St.), Life of. By Rev. T. Meyrick. 12mo., 2s.
What Catholics do not Believe. By Bishop Ryan. 12mo., 1s.
WENINGER(Rev.F.X.,S.J.),LivesoftheSaintsforevery
day in the Year. Illustrated. 4to., 2 vols., or 12 vols., 50s.
WHITE (George), Cardinal Wiseman. 12mo., 1s. and 1s. 6d.
——— Comte de Montalembert. 12mo., 6d.
——— Life of S. Edmund of Canterbury. 1s. and 1s. 6d.
——— Pius IX., from his Birth to his Death. 12mo., 6d.
William (St.), of York. A Drama in Two Acts. (Boys.) 12mo., 6d.
WILLIAMS (Canon), Anglican Orders. 12mo., 3s. 6d.
Wiseman (Cardinal), Life and Obsequies. 1s. and 1s. 6d.
——— Recollections of. By M. J. Arnold. 12mo., 2s. 6d.
WOODS (Canon), Defence of the Roman Church against
F. Gratry. Translated from the French of Gueranger. 1s. 6d.
WYATT-EDGELL (Alfred), Stormsworth, with other Poems
and Plays. 12mo., 3s. 6d.
——— Thy Gods! O Israel. 12mo., 2s.
Young Catholic's Guide to Confession and Holy Com-
munion. By Dr. Kenny. 32mo., 4d.; cloth, 6d.; red edges, 9d.,
French morocco, 1s. 6d.; calf or morocco, 2s. 6d.
YOUNG (T., Esq.), History of Ireland. 18mo., 2s. 6d.
Zouaves, Pontifical, Two Years in. By Joseph Powell, Z.P.
Illustrated. 8vo., 3s. 6d.

R. Washbourne, 18 Paternoster Row, London.

PRAYER BOOKS.

Garden, Little, of the Soul. Edited by the Rev. R. G. Davis. *With Imprimatur of the Archbishop of Westminster.* This book, as its name imports, contains a selection from the "Garden of the Soul" of the Prayers and Devotions of most general use. Whilst it will serve as a *Pocket Prayer Book* for all, it is, by its low price, *par excellence*, the Prayer Book for children and for the very poor. In it are to be found the old familiar Devotions of the "Garden of the Soul," as well as many important additions, such as the Devotions to the Sacred Heart, to Saint Joseph, to the Guardian Angels, and others. The omissions are mainly the Forms of administering the Sacraments, and Devotions that are not of very general use. It is printed in a clear type, on a good paper, both especially selected, for the purpose of obviating the disagreeableness of small type and inferior paper. Fifteenth Thousand.

    32mo., price, cloth, 6d.; with rims, 1s. Embossed, red edges, 9d.; with rims and clasp, 1s. 3d.; Strong roan, 1s.; with rims and clasp, 1s. 6d. French morocco, 1s. 6d.; with rims and clasp, 2s. French morocco extra gilt, 2s.; with rims and clasp, 2s. 6d. Calf or morocco, 3s.; with rims and clasp, 4s. Calf or morocco, extra gilt, 4s.; with rims and clasp, 5s. Morocco antique, 7s. 6d., 10s. 6d., 12s., 16s. Velvet, rims and clasp, 5s., 8s. 6d., and 10s. 6d. Russia, 5s.; with clasp, &c., 8s. ; Russia antique, 17s. 6d. Ivory, with rims and clasp, 10s. 6d., 13s., 15s., 17s. 6d. Imitation ivory, with rims and clasp, 3s. With oxydized silver or gilt mountings, in morocco case, 25s.

Catholic Hours: a Manual of Prayer, including Mass and Vespers. By J. R. Digby Beste, Esq. 32mo., cloth, 2s.; red edges, 2s. 6d.; roan, 3s.; morocco, 6s.

Catholic Piety; or, Key of Heaven, with Epistles and Gospels. Large 32mo., roan, 1s. 6d. and 2s.; French morocco, with rims and clasp, 2s. 6d.; extra gilt, 3s.; with rims and clasp, 3s. 6d.

Catholic Piety; or, Key of Heaven. 32mo., 6d.; rims and clasp, 1s.; French morocco, 1s.; velvet, with rims and clasp, 2s. 6d.; with Epistles and Gospels, roan, 1s.; French morocco, 1s. 6d.; with rims and clasp, 2s.; extra gilt, 2s.; Persian, 2s. 6d.; imitation ivory, 3s.; morocco, 3s. 6d.; velvet, rims and clasp, 3s. 6d.

Crown of Jesus. 18mo., Persian calf, 6s. Calf or Morocco, 7s. 6d. and 8s. 6d.; with rims and clasp, 10s. 6d. Calf or morocco, extra gilt, 10s. 6d.; with rims and clasp, 12s. 6d; with turn-over edges, 10s. 6d. Ivory, with rims and clasp, 21s., 25s., 27s. 6d. and 30s.

Daily Exercises for Devout Christians. By Rev. P. V. Monk, O.S.B. 18mo., 3s. 6d.

Devotions for Mass. Very large type, 12mo., 2d.

Garden of the Soul. Very large Type. 18mo., cloth, 1s.; with Epistles and Gospels, 1s. 6d.; French morocco, 2s. 6d.; with E. and G., 3s. 6d. Best edition, without E. and G., 3s. 6d.; with E. and G., morocco circuit, 7s. 6d.; calf antique, with clasp, 8s.; French morocco, antique, with clasp, 6s. 6d.

    Epistles and Gospels, in French morocco, 2s.

R. Washbourne, 18 *Paternoster Row, London.*

Holy Childhood. Simple Prayers for very little children. 32mo., 1s.; gilt, 1s. 6d.; cheap edition, 6d.
Illustrated Manual of Prayers. 32mo., 3d.; cloth, 4d.
Key of Heaven. *Very large type.* 18mo., 1s.; leather, 2s. 6d.
Lily of St. Joseph, The; a little Manual of Prayers and Hymns for Mass. 64mo., price 2d.; cloth, 3d., 4d., 6d., or 8d.; roan, 1s.; French morocco, 1s. 6d.; calf or morocco, 2s.; gilt, 2s. 6d.
Little Prayer Book, The, for Ordinary Catholic Devotions. 3d.
Manual of Catholic Devotions. Small, for the waistcoat pocket. 64mo., 6d.; with Epistles and Gospels, cloth, 6d.; with rims, 1s.; roan, 1s.; with tuck, 1s. 6d.; calf or morocco, 2s. 6d.; ivorine, 2s. 6d.
Manual of Devotions in Honour of our Lady of Sorrows. 18mo., 1s. 6d.; cheaper binding, 1s.
Manual of the Sisters of Charity. 18mo., 6s.
Memorare Mass. By Sister M. F. Clare, of Kenmare. 32mo., 2d.
Missal (Complete). 18mo., Persian, 8s. 6d.; calf or morocco, 10s. 6d.; with rims and clasp, 13s. 6d.; calf or mor., extra gilt, 12s. 6d., with rims and clasp, 15s. 6d.; morocco, with turn-over edges, 13s. 6d.; morocco antique, 15s.; velvet, 20s.; Russia, 20s.; ivory, with rims and clasp, 31s. 6d. and 35s.
——— A very beautiful edition, handsomely bound in morocco, gilt mountings, silk linings, edges red on gold, in a morocco case. Illustrated, £5. [clasp, 8s.
Missal and Vesper Book, in one vol. 32mo., morocco, 6s.; with
Occasional Prayers for Festivals. 4d. and 6d.; gilt, 1s.
OREMUS, A Liturgical Prayer Book : with the Imprimatur of the Cardinal Archbishop of Westminster. An adaptation of the Church Offices : containing Morning and Evening Devotions ; Devotion for Mass, Confession, and Communion, and various other Devotions ; Common and Proper, Hymns, Lessons, Collects, Epistles and Gospels for Sundays, Feasts, and Week Days ; and short notices of over 200 Saints' Days. 32mo., 452 pages, 2s. ; cloth, 2s. 6d.; embossed, red edges, 3s. 6d.; French morocco, 4s. 6d.; calf, 5s. 6d.; morocco, 6s.; Russia, 8s. 6d., &c., &c., &c.
Path to Paradise. 32 full-page Illustrations. 32mo., cloth, 3d. With 50 Illustrations, cloth, 4d. Superior edition, 6d. and 1s.
Serving Boy's Manual and Book of Catholic Devotions, containing all those Prayers and Devotions for Sundays and Holidays, usually divided in their recitation between the Priest and the Congregation. Compiled from approved sources, and adapted to Churches served either by the Secular or the Regular Clergy, 32mo., Embossed, 1s.; with Epistles and Gospels, 1s. 6d.; French morocco, 2s., with Epistles and Gospels, 2s. 6d.; calf, 4s., with Epistles and Gospels, 4s. 6d.
Soul united to Jesus in the Adorable Sacrament. 1s. 6d.
S. Patrick's Manual. Compiled by Sister Mary Frances Clare. 3s. 6d.
Sure Way to Heaven. Cloth, 6d.: Persian, 2s. 6d.; morocco, 3s. 6d.
Treasury of the Sacred Heart. 18mo., 3s. 6d.; roan, 4s. 6d. 32mo., 2s.; French morocco, 2s. 6d.; calf 5s.; morocco, 6s.
Ursuline Manual. 18mo., 4s.; Persian calf, 7s. 6d.; morocco, 10s.

R. Washbourne, 18 Paternoster Row, London.

Garden of the Soul. (WASHBOURNE'S EDITION.) Edited by the Rev. R. G. Davis. *With Imprimatur of the Archbishop of Westminster.* Twentieth Thousand. This Edition retains all the Devotions that have made the GARDEN OF THE SOUL, now for many generations, the well-known Prayer-book for English Catholics. During many years various Devotions have been introduced, and, in the form of appendices, have been added to other editions. These have now been incorporated into the body of the work, and, together with the Devotions to the Sacred Heart, to Saint Joseph, to the Guardian Angels, the Itinerarium, and other important additions, render this edition pre-eminently the Manual of Prayer, for both public and private use. The version of the Psalms has been carefully revised, and strictly conformed to the Douay translation of the Bible, published with the approbation of the LATE CARDINAL WISEMAN. The Forms of administering the Sacraments have been carefully translated, *as also the rubrical directions,* from the Ordo Administrandi Sacramenta. To enable all present, either at baptisms or other public administrations of the Sacraments, to pay due attention to the sacred rites, the Forms are inserted without any curtailment, both in Latin and English. The Devotions at Mass have been carefully revised, and enriched by copious adaptations from the prayers of the Missal. The preparation for the Sacraments of Penance and the Holy Eucharist have been the objects of especial care, to adapt them to the wants of those whose religious instruction may be deficient. Great attention has been paid to the quality of the paper and to the size of type used in the printing, to obviate that weariness so distressing to the eyes, caused by the use of books printed in small close type and on inferior paper.

32mo. Embossed, 1s.; with rims and clasp, 1s. 6d.; with Epistles and Gospels, 1s. 6d.; with rims and clasp, 2s. French morocco, 2s.; with rims and clasp, 2s. 6d.; with E. and G., 2s. 6d.; with rims and clasp, 3s. French morocco extra gilt, 2s. 6d.; with rims and clasp, 3s.; with E. and G., 3s.; with rims and clasp, 3s. 6d. Calf, or morocco 4s.; with rims and clasp, 5s. 6d.; with E. and G., 4s. 6d., with rims and clasp, 6s. Calf or morocco extra gilt, 5s.; with rims and 'clasp, 6s. 6d.; with E. and G., 5s. 6d.; with rims and clasp, 7s. Velvet, with rims and clasp, 6d., 10s. 6d., and 13s.; with E. and G., 8s., 11s., and 13s. 6d. Russia, antique, with clasp, 8s. 6d., 10s., 12s. 6d.; with E. and G., 9s. 10s. 6d., 13s., with corners and clasps, 20s.; with E. and G., 20s. 6d. Ivory 14s., 16s., 18s., 20s., and 22s. 6d.; with E. and G., 14s. 6d., 16s. 6d., 18s. 6d., 20s. 6d., and 23s. Morocco antique, with 2 patent clasps, 12s.; with E. and G., 12s. 6d.; with corners and clasps, 18s.; with E. and G., 18s. 6d.

The Epistles and Gospels. *Complete,* cloth, 6d.; roan, 1s. 6d.

"This is one of the best editions we have seen of one of the best of all our Prayer Books. It is well printed in clear, large type, on good paper."—*Catholic Opinion.*

A very complete arrangement of this which is emphatically the Prayer Book of every Catholic household. It is as cheap as it is good, and we heartily recommend it."—*Universe.* "Two striking features are the admirable order displayed throughout the book, and the insertion of the Indulgences in small type above Indulgenced Prayers. In the Devotions for Mass, the editor has, with great discrimination, drawn largely on the Church's Prayers, as given us in the Missal."—*Weekly Register.*

R. Washbourne, 18 Paternoster Row, London.

www.ingramcontent.com/pod-product-compliance
Lightning Source LLC
Chambersburg PA
CBHW022135160426
43197CB00009B/1290